The
LADIES' GUIDE
to
NEEDLE WORK

*being a complete guide
to all types of*

LADIES' FANCY WORK

by

S. Annie Frost

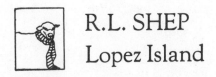

R.L. SHEP
Lopez Island

TT
750
F76
1986

This edition is an unabridged reproduction of the original which was first published in 1877.

ISBN 0-914046-02-0
LC# 85-090544

Printed in the United States of America

Published by:

R.L. SHEP
Box C-20
LOPEZ ISLAND,
Washington 98261

THE LADIES' GUIDE

TO

ETC.,

By S. ANNIE FROST.

BEING A COMPLETE GUIDE TO ALL KINDS OF

Ladies' Fancy Work,

WITH FULL DESCRIPTIONS OF ALL THE VARIOUS STITCHES AND MATERIALS, AND A LARGE NUMBER OF ILLUSTRATIONS FOR EACH VARIETY OF WORK.

ADAMS & BISHOP, Publishers,

46 Beekman Street,

NEW YORK.

Table of Contents

will be found on pages 155-158

INTRODUCTION.

———•••———

NEEDLEWORK.

There is no occupation so essentially feminine, at the same time so truly lady-like, as needlework in every branch, from the plain, useful sewing that keeps household and person neat and orderly, to the exquisite, dainty fancy work that adds beauty to every room.

From the earliest age women of every rank have employed themselves with needlework in every variety, and some of the specimens still extant of old-time embroidery and lace-work excite the wonder as well as the admiration of all beholders, being marvels not only of skill but of patience.

Spinning, weaving, tapestry, lace-work and embroidery, have all been women's work since those primitive times when the mistress sat among her maids in her chamber, controlling and directing their work, while busily employed upon her own. Fancy as well as fact dates the use of the needle to the remotest ages, for the rivalry of Minerva and Arachne, and the wondrous webs they wove, are in every mythology, and all are familiar with the stories of the webs woven by Penelope and Philomela.

The sisters of King Ethelstan were famous for their skill in spinning, weaving, and embroidery, their father having educated them to give their entire attention to letters first, and afterwards to the distaff and needle. The queen of Edward the Confessor was well known as an expert needlewoman, and the celebrated Bayeaux tapestry, worked by the wife of the Conqueror, is a grand proof of what can be done with that feminine implement, the needle.

Martha Washington received her lady friends, rising from her knitting or sewing, and resuming the work of her fingers while conversing, and there are specimens of her skill still treasured.

Too much cannot be said in favor of this branch of feminine education, and it is a grievous error to allow girls to arrive at maturity ignorant of the full use of the needle. It should be introduced into the daily routine of every school, more especially the plainer and more useful branches, and as early as possible every girl should be required to make and keep in perfect repair the articles in her own wardrobe.

Fancy work is a secondary consideration, although this little book will be for the guidance of those, who, having conquered the mysteries of plain sewing, turn for recreation to the daintier and prettier arts of embroidery and fancy knitting.

The march of progress extends into this domain as well as all others, and every day some new fancy is displayed in needlework simply for ornamentation. But while the variety of form and use is endless, close examination will generally prove to the expert needlewoman that the most complicated and bewildering combinations reduce themselves to some simple stitch or rule perfectly familiar to them, and the embroidery, crochet, or knitting needle already in possession is the only implement required.

The stores for the sale of fancy work, also supply every variety of material carefully prepared for use, simplifying every branch of needlework. To attempt to describe every article in detail would far exceed the compass of this little volume, but the rules and directions here given will be found to contain the foundation for one and all of the new devices.

CHAPTER I.

EMBROIDERY.

The word embroidery covers the largest and most varied of all fancy work, while comprising the most elegant and artistic effects. In colors it is truly needle-painting, since the combination and shading require the taste and skill of an artist to design and execute. Flowers, birds and arabesque patterns with infinite varieties of grouping are the favorite patterns, and are supplied in all fancy stores where they are stamped upon the material.

Cotton Embroidery.

is used principally for the trimming of undergarments, though much in vogue now for linen and cambric dresses and for children's suits. Many kinds of stitches are required, the most used of all, being

Button-hole Stitch.

This is used for the edges of all kinds of cotton embroidery, and the stamped patterns have a variety of points and scallops, the lines of which are to be carefully followed in this manner: Between the upper and lower lines run three or four rows of embroidery cotton, in long, loose stitches, to give the work a rich, raised appearance. When this is done, put the point of the needle into the upper line, passing it under to come out upon the lower line; the thread must be held with the thumb of the left hand under the needle point, so as to be confined in a loop when the stitch is taken. A succession of such loops forms the edge called button-hole stitch.

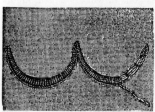

Fig. 1.—BUTTON-HOLE STITCH.

The entire beauty of scallops and points so worked consists in their being perfectly even, and this can be attained only by following the lines of the pattern with the most careful accuracy. Scallops can be made with one clear edge or with the inside curve clear, and the outside one graduated in smaller curves. Either forms a pretty finish to muslin embroidery, the first being easiest to work evenly.

Eyelet Holes

are extensively used in cotton embroidery, and require practice and care to work prettily and evenly. The plain eyelet hole is pierced first with a stiletto and worked over and over in very close, even stitches. Graduated eyelets have a double circle upon one side, and this must be worked in longer stitches, and care taken not to draw the thread tightly. If large, the double line should be filled in with long, loose stitches, as the scallops are filled.

Fig. 2.—EYELET HOLES.

Satin Stitch

is the long stit;h that follows the pattern of leaves, flowers and figures, by filling the spaces between the lines. This space must be first carefully crossed and re-crossed by long threads running in the contrary way from those designed to cover them, being put in to

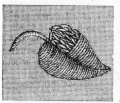

give the work the proper raised appearance. When this is done, the working stitches, very close and fine, must follow the pattern carefully, with a perfectly even edge. Leaves must have the threads starting from the centre of the veining and running out to the points in every case, never worked across, as they will certainly appear uneven. The veining should be carefully marked, but never stitched, as it is properly defined by the meeting of the satin stitches. Flowers must be w rked from the centre, every petal separately, each being properly defined if the

Fig. 3.—SATIN STITCH.   satin stitch is even and close.

Spot Stitch

is used for dots only, large or small, the cotton being carried across the stamped circle twice, one row of stitches laying over the other.

Minute Stitch

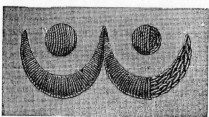

is used for exceedingly small dots, and is done in what is called minute cotton, very coarse. It is merely a short back stitch covering the tiny stamped dot, the cotton passing on the wrong side from one dot to another.

Fig. 4.—SPOT STITCH.

With a perfect knowledge of these stitches all the varieties of cotton embroidery can be worked, the English embroidery being usually in less elaborate patterns than the French.

Patterns are stamped for a trifle at all fancy stores, and where they can be so procured are usually more accurate than those traced over impression paper, or upon thin muslin.

The thread must be graduated according to the fine or coarse texture of the material to be embroidered, and where linen is used, linen thread will be found both handsome and durable.

Fig. 5.—MINUTE STITCH.   In embroidering initials, borders or corners for pocket handkerchiefs, the finest thread must be selected, and great care taken to keep the wrong as well as the right side of the work perfectly even. Leaves and flowers in handkerchief embroidery are very effective if worked upon one side of the veining in satin stitch, and upon the other in very fine dots close together. In this very fine work, the veining is frequently worked after the flower or leaf is filled in, with a close over-stitch. Lines, such as stems of flowers, must be followed in a very fine close over-stitch, slanting one thread only from a straight line. Care must be taken to raise but little of the material with the needle, no more being taken up than will suffice to hold the embroidery thread smooth and firm.

In French embroidery there is frequently introduced the

Wheel Stitch.

The wheels are cut out with a pair of fine embroidery scissors, and the space

filled with long threads knotted by a loop stitch to form a small, even circle in the centre, from which the threads radiate to a strongly-worked edge. There are many patterns, and the stitch requires great practice, as the beauty is gone if there is the slightest uneven appearance in edge, centre or the thread spokes.

Fig. 6.
WHEEL STITCH.

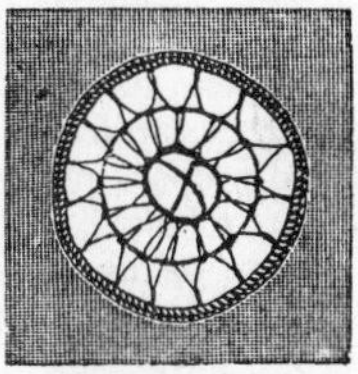

Fig. 7.
WHEEL STITCH.

Herring-Bone Stitch

is extensively used in cotton embroidery for children's aprons and ornamenting cheap garments where there is not time for embroidery. It is done by alternating loops and long stitches and sewing backwards. Patterns are stamped, but every needlewoman understands following a seam or hem in herring-bone.

Chain Stitch

is also an easy stitch, formed by holding the thread firmly over the point of the needle while it is drawn out, so as to form a loop. The needle is set back into the centre of this loop, and the thread again

Fig. 8.
HERRING-BONE STITCH.

passed over the point to form a second one, and so on, the succession of loops forming the chain. Braiding patterns worked in chain stitch, in colored cotton, are very effective and will wash and wear better than the braid.

Cotton embroidery is always fashionable for undergarments, handkerchiefs, housekeeping linen and children's clothing.

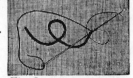

Fig. 9.—CHAIN STITCH.

Necktie End in Embroidery.

This can be worked upon fine Swiss or French muslin, the end hemmed, or if preferred, worked in a button-hole stitch scallop. The work is satin stitch, excepting the middle of the large leaves, which are worked in spot stitch, well raised.

Handkerchief Corner,

to be worked in satin and minute stitch, with either hemstitched or button-hole scallop border.

Silk and Wool Embroidery

may come under the same head, as they are frequently used in combination, and are done upon the same materials and in the same manner.

Both require a frame in order to be perfectly worked, and great care is necessary in adjusting both frame and work. The standing frame is the best, being adjustable by means of screws which raise or lower it to the height desired. But table frames can be used, and for small pieces of work the lap frame is very convenient.

To prepare work for a frame it should be strongly bound with coarse muslin or linen to baste to the webbing that should be attached to the frame. When the material to be embroidered is strongly bound, it must be basted into the frame with the selvages at the sides, by threads that are sufficiently strong to hold it firmly in place. If too long for the frame, roll the material at the top, and fasten the roll firmly with strong threads.

Fig. 10.—NECKTIE FND.

The materials for silk or wool embroidery are velvet, satin, silk, cloth, and at this time ticking and crash, both of which have been lately discovered to make an effective background for the bright colors of embroidery silk and zephyr.

The patterns to be worked must be first carefully stamped or traced upon the material, and the colors of the embroidery silk carefully selected and shaded, shades being artistically toned so as not to offend the eye by violent contrast.

In embroidering flowers and leaves, the best rule is to follow the natural colors as nearly as possible, using the various greens for foliage as they would occur in the bouquet of real flowers.

Long stitches must be used, starting invariably from the centre of leaf or flower near the stem, where the darkest shades should be employed, shading to lighter ones near the edges. The stitches must vary in length to follow the pattern, and must be close and perfectly even, to produce a good effect. Leaves must be worked outward from centre stem to the points, and always lengthwise, and the veining should be worked in, always in a darker shade than that

22399

Fig. 11.—HANDKERCHIEF CORNER.

employed in working the leaves. Stems should be worked in darker shades than leaves or flowers, and browns are very effective. The stitch for stems should slant lengthwise slightly, excepting where the stem is thick, when it should be worked straight across.

All leaves and petals should be done in satin stitch, carefully filled by long crosswise stitches of the same silk as that used for working.

If the work is done in shaded silks, which can now be obtained in every color, of the best quality, care must be taken to match the shades exactly when joining on new stitches, or the effect will be broken and patched. But if carefully used in this respect, the shaded silk is very effective and much less trouble in working.

Knotted Embroidery.

In forming knots for embroidery, for the centre of flowers or arabesque work, bring the needle up in the spot where you wish to place the knot. Wind the silk twice round the needle and push it down in exactly the spot where it was pushed up. Let the silk be drawn through slowly, being careful it does not tangle, and the twist around the needle will form the knot. It requires some practice to do knotted embroidery well, but it can be introduced with good effect into many kinds of silk embroidery.

Raised Embroidery,

in silk or wool, is made by covering the space to be worked with very fine jeweller's cotton, which is tacked down on the edges. It must be entirely covered with stitches close together, sewed across, and this again covered by satin stitch.

Another form of raised embroidery is called tufted work, but can be done only in wools. The darkest shade is worked like the stem work, only in stitches straight across and very close together. The next shade is worked over the first, but the needle is not passed across underneath, but takes a very tiny stitch first on one side and then on the other over and over until the first stitches are covered. The shades are thus worked in one after another, each one as close as possible to the line of the last until the lightest shade covers all. Then the whole is cut through, exactly in the middle, and the tufts form themselves. Dahlias, birds, animals' heads, and shells, are very handsome worked in this way.

A new and most beautiful style of embroidery has lately been introduced into this country, an imitation of

Turkish Embroidery.

It is worked upon very fine thick cloth in every shade and color, from the palest neutral tints to black. The patterns are stamped, and consist of lines similar to those used in braiding, forming graceful designs, according to the use for which they are to be adapted. These lines are followed in a very fine close chain stitch in bright-hued silks of every color, harmoniously blended and contrasted. The effect is very rich and beautiful, and the work is in great favor. Chair coverings, foot-stools, table-cloths, lambrequins, and a great variety of household ornamentation is done in the Turkish embroidery, and when it is evenly worked it cannot be distinguished from the imported work. Gold and silver thread may be introduced with good effect, but has the fault of tarnishing very soon.

Slippers, smoking-caps, pincushions and many small articles are worked in

Turkish embroidery upon velvet, satin, or silk, and are new and fashionable. Flowers and leaves may be so worked by filling the spaces with fine close rows of chain stitching, but the effect is not so good as in arabesque patterns.

Crash Embroidery

is another fashionable freak for tidies, sofa cushions, and other articles. It is very easily done, and very effective. The crash must be of linen, with the pattern stamped upon it. It is usually a large star. This must be filled, and worked across in shaded zephyr, each star in a different color, or the colors arranged to form lines, diamonds, blocks, or circles. After the embroidery is done, the edge must be fringed by knotting in lengths of the zephyr, or if preferred, an edge can be worked in button-hole stitch scallops. The very coarse crash is not so effective for a background as a finer quality, and the darker shades of lead color are the best contrast to the gay zephyr. Tidies of this work are very useful as they are strong, wear well, and do not soil easily.

Fig. 12.—CASE FOR BOOK (OPEN).

Fig. 13.—CASE FOR BOOK (CLOSED).

Case for Book.

This case may be used to preserve a book in travelling, or a choicely-bound volume in the library. The case may be of cloth or holland, according to taste. It is ornamented with a simple pattern in embroidery in silk of any color, and is bound with sarcenet ribbon. The back, front, flap, and sides are cut in one piece, and the sides are joined to the back. The case must be cut to the size of the book for which it is intended. It is fastened with a band of elastic, and straps are put on to carry it by.

Ticking Embroidery

is another fashionable freak. The material which is used for bedding, would have been, one might suppose, the last thing to form the groundwork of ladies' fancy work, but the effect is excellent. Coarse colored netting silk and gold braid are all that is needed besides the ticking to embroider a pair of slippers which will have the effect of Moorish work. Between the stripes of the ticking a coral stitch must be worked, alternating with herring-bone stitch, the gold braid being run on between the black stripes of the ticking with very fine gold-colored silk. Being very easy and inexpensive, this is a work in which even a little girl could soon produce a pair of slippers handsomer than wool work, and wearing equally well.

The celebrated authoress Jean Ingelow contributes to an English magazine the following description of some specimens of needlework, which will give my readers some useful hints and instructions in embroidery. She writes:

"You were saying the other day that you should like to have a description from me of some of the kinds of needlework that we possess which are either peculiar or pretty.

"Of these I think a pair of pictures of dead game, worked by my aunt, after Miss Linwood's style, come first. They are seldom noticed by our friends for the simple reason that they always pass for oil paintings; but when closely inspected as they hang on the wall, every stitch is visible. They are not done on canvass, and are neither in tapestry stitch nor square stitch, but in a long irregular stitch. Here and there shadows have been worked in as an after thought, or deeper tints have been laid over the already worked ground. The stitches in the birds' heads are almost as fine as touches in a miniature; but a falling feather, which seems to be coming down as lightly as a snow-flake, shows on investigation that the whole ground of the picture was finished before it was worked on, and the stitches forming it go across and over the other.

"These pictures have been worked about seventy years, and are as fresh as ever. They may almost be called works of art, instead of which the lamb's-wool work generally done can rank no higher than the merest ornament, and it does not last ten years.

"I think any one who has a knowledge of drawing and a picture to copy might easily do this work.

"When a child, I sometimes heard my old aunt describe the process. Mrs. Linwood, mother of the celebrated Miss Linwood, had a school at Leicester, and the daughter gave lessons in it, on this peculiar work. My aunt was educated by Mrs. Linwood. She showed a remarkable aptitude for painting thus with the needle, but unluckily she regarded the art as a mere accomplishment, and hardly ever troubled herself to exercise it after she left school.

"The two pictures are all we have of her doing. She told my mother they were worked in a frame on a stiff twilled material called 'tammy.' An outline of the picture to be copied was drawn in chalk, and the worker stood at her frame, and retired every few minutes to observe the effect from a distance. No stitches were ever pulled out, but worked over.

"Miss Linwood employed a special dyer to make innumerable shades of colors for her. She used either a harsh thin worsted, or a very fine crewel. Lamb's-wool and silk will not do, as they fade. Any one who has a taste for drawing, and a good oil painting for a copy, might work a picture thus. It is, of course, understood that the whole ground is to be carefully worked over. Landscapes look remarkably well, fruit and flower pieces, also birds and most animals.

"Then I must mention a kind of work that my mother often does, and that you admired. Many years ago an aunt of mine was describing to my mother some work she had seen done at Taunton. It was satin-stitch embroidery, cut out, arranged in some kind of regular pattern, and the interstices connected together with a net work of fine crochet. I may as well remark in passing that satin stitch, however old and worn the fabric may be from which it is cut, does not fray; it remains intact and hard. My mother cut out the satin stitch patterns from some old India muslin gowns, babies' caps and robes, and instead of connecting it with crochet, made a very much richer and far handsomer fabric with it thus:

Fig. 14.—EMBROIDERY.

"She took a piece of stiff writing paper, and with a needle and thread fastened down upon it the cut-out work, face downward. She took care to use such a variety of forms and sizes that no regular pattern could be traced in the work. At some point or other each piece of satin stitch touched the next. A great deal of the richness of the effect was found to depend on there not being too much groundwork. A very fine thread was then drawn from point to point of the satin stitch, and worked over in button-hole stitch till the whole was quite secure, so that in wearing no point could rise, the fabric being firm enough to be cut away from the paper. We generally make this work in pieces about as large as the palm of the hand, and put them together afterwards. This insures their being perfectly clean. The effect is more beautiful than most kinds of ancient lace, and the fabric is very durable, a large berthe made by my mother twenty-five years ago being still in perfectly good condition, though it has been very much worn.

"Of course the beauty depends partly on the richness and variety of the work used. Any one can make it who has satin-stitch patterns to cut out; but I must repeat that the fine effect greatly depends on the endless intricacies of the pattern, and this is an accidental perfection, depending upon there being plenty of work to select from, and from the carefulness of the worker to avoid repetition. Several people, friends of our own, who have copied this work, have been induced, on the contrary, to make a decided pattern. This is always found to spoil the effect.

"My mother invented another kind of needlework, but neither she nor I can describe it; for it is done without any pattern, and must be invented by the worker as she goes on. The annexed drawing may assist.

"The fabric is cloth, and the flowers are worked in wool in their natural colors."

Roman Embroidery

is one of the new devices for combinations of stitches. It is done on stout brown linen, which comes in the fancy stores already stamped for every suitable article, such as screens, comb-bags, pin-cushions, watch-pockets, or other trifles. It is worked with a brown linen thread that comes especially for this use. The principal stitch is button-hole, and the object of the work is to make the edge of the button-hole stitch meet in the pattern, and wherever it does so a piece of the linen is cut out. Care must be taken not to cut where the button-hole stitch does not meet. The centres of the pattern are done in satin stitch. After the work is finished and cut out, silk of any color should be put underneath, the brighter the better, as the design is then well thrown out.

A very handsome piece of this work was made into a shawl bag for travelling, the brown linen and embroidery being made over French cambric, highly glossed, of a deep rich crimson, the buttons being covered with the cambric, and the edges button-hole stitched with crimson thread to match.

Mediæval Embroidery

is another popular fancy. It is done in crewells, or fine Berlin wool, the first being the best for articles requiring washing, the latter the most effective. The designs are, as the name infers, from the old tapestries. They are traced on linen by means of transfer paper, and then a line is worked round the margin in black chain stitch, and each petal or portion of design is filled up with chain stitch in one shade. The stalks are made by using double crewell and bringing the needle out between the two threads. The work is very durable, and is handsome and easily done.

Embroidery after Nature.

This style of work is often called "painting in wools." It consists of working flowers in their natural forms and colors, and can only be done by persons who have a knowledge of painting. First, the flower must be drawn boldly on the piece of coarse unbleached linen.

The margin of the petal is worked in long close stitches, making a firm, thick edge, half an inch deep, the threads lying in the direction of the veins of the petal. Other shades are then worked in, to fill up the petal, in long unequal stitches, care being taken to bring the needle up in the middle of the threads forming the margin, so as to blend the work and make all smooth. Both in leaves and flowers it is necessary to place the stitches in the direction of the veining. When the flower is worked, veins in a darker shade can be added, if the nature of the bloom requires them, or spots of any size or shade. Middles are worked in the knotting stitch already described. If great care is taken not to draw the hand tight in the working, no anxiety need be felt as to the apparent puckering. When the work is finished, it must be stretched, face downwards, on a board, and strongly starched at the back; then dried quickly and removed, when the effect will satisfy the most fastidious judge. The flowers stand up from the ground, which is now quite flat, and really seem as if they could be taken up. A country woman, seeing furniture covered with this work exclaimed, " Why, surely, it is a flower garden."

Ladies who do this work become wholly fascinated by it, and it is quickly done, as well as being so effective. Sometimes a groundwork is added of feather stitch in black machine silk. This has the effect of a tracery background, neither heightening the effect of the flowers nor detracting from it, but disguising the roughness of the material and preventing its soiling so quickly.

Chinese Embroidery.

These specimens of needlework, requiring great skill and care in execution, are usually framed when finished, and we give a drawing, as they are difficult to describe. The work from which it is copied is on black satin, very thick and glossy.

Fig. 15.—CHINESE EMBROIDERY.

The birds are brilliantly colored and worked in fine floss silk in long irregular stitches, one being vivid shades of blue, the other scarlet. The foliage is of very bright and dark green artistically blended, and the finer dots are of gold thread. The spots are in red and white silk worked over and over.

Feather Embroidery.

The piece of stuff, cloth, net, muslin, or velvet, which you would embroider, must be stitched into a frame, and the design traced on it. Having selected the feathers of such colors as you require for the flower or bird you wish to represent, take a paint brush and carefully cover the inside of them with green; when dry,

Fig. 16.—LAMP-MAT IN FEATHER EMBROIDERY.

cut them with a sharp pair of scissors, in the shape of the petals or leaves required; this being done, take a needle threaded with fine silk of the color of the feather and secure it to the design, carefully fastening the ends of the silk. This embroidery is very beautiful, and is rare, owing to the difficulty of procuring small, high-colored feathers.

Another method of embroidering in feathers is to sew them one over the other, covering the edges of the last row with embroidery, fringe, quilted ribbon, or any other trimming.

The following illustration is a lamp mat upon net canvas, in feather embroidery.

Fig. 17.—PATTERN TO SHOW HOW THE FEATHERS ARE FASTENED.

The ends of the feathers are slipped through the meshes of the net, to the wrong side, and securely fastened. The edge consists of three rows of feathers, two rows of quilled ribbon, and the centre of the mat grounded in a dark color, or, if preferred, a pattern can be embroidered in silk or Berlin wool upon the net.

Embroidery in Narrow Ribbon.

The ribbons to be used are the narrow shaded ones to be bought at most dry goods shops. The design is traced upon the material to be worked, and as each stitch forms a petal or leaf, the design must not be too elaborate; small rosettes and flowers are prettier than large ones. The ribbon is to be threaded through a large wool needle, and worked as you would silk or wool. For the stems, tendrils, centres of flowers, etc., colored silk must be used.

Table or Mantelpiece Bordering.

Take a piece of common linen stair-covering, cut off the border (take care the pattern is a good flowery one); work the leaves of the pattern with different shades of green, single Berlin wool, in a long embroidery stitch. Buttonhole the flowers, some with different colors—crimson, bright pink, lilac, and blue; work the centre eye of the flower in black wool, stitch the black wool down at intervals with yellow purse-silk, and make rays of the yellow silk and the wool in sets of three long stitches from the eye to the buttonhole border, which should be a zig-

Fig. 18.

zag, should be in four shades of brown, beginning from pale maize and finishing with an outside one of black, large stitches of yellow silk caught over each point of the border.

Rug Worked on Sackcloth.

This mat is worked upon common corn-sacking, and the length required for a rug is about a yard and a half or three-quarters, according to taste, and the cost is about one shilling and six pence for the piece necessary. It was first seen in Ireland, but who first introduced the idea is not known. The sacking requires first to be well cleansed of the little uneven discolored bits of sacking, by pulling them out, and when that is finished, you begin by No. 19, working a common herring-bone in yellow wool round the edge of the sacking, as seen in the illustration. As much care as possible must be made to keep the herring-bone equal in size. No. 20 is the same stitch, but worked in black wool. Two rows all round the mat must be worked, and eventually crossed like the illustration, and then the corners are formed by working eight stitches or squares above the double row of black, beginning from the corner stitch. Continue working these eight stitches, one row upon the other, till a complete square is formed, allowing you to count eight stitches on each side of the square. Make one of these squares at each corner of the sacking, after which the points round the mat must be worked, and that can only be done by counting how many squares or stitches there are between

No. 19.

No. 20.

each corner, and how many stitches can be reserved for each point, leaving one or two stitches between, and graduating the squares or stitches to a point, as shown in the illustration.

No. 21.

After having completed the large squares at the corners and the points, comes No. 21, a star in red (double) wool, with a centre of double yellow wool, which is made in the centre of each corner and each point, those of the corners being much larger.

No. 22 consists of stars worked in single wool of various colors, according to taste, one being placed above each black point, and one between them. Then make a centre to each star, in black, as shown in the illustration; after which put a star of yellow wool over the black centre, except to the yellow stars, which remain black. These centres are made in single wool.

No. 22.

No. 23.

No. 24 is simply a large herring-bone stitch pointed with black, and caught in the centre with yellow, like the illustration. This is worked in red or magenta, and forms the first row of the centre of the mat, and must of necessity be worked at an equal distance from the corners.

No. 25 is worked in red, black and green, like the illustration, just a little above No. 24.

No. 26 is a kind of rainbow of colors, placed as seen in the illustration, worked in single wool. After this is finished, place your five stars (two yellow, two blue, and a red) in the centre at equal distance from each other, and work them exactly as you did those in No. 22.

No. 24.

No. 25.

No. 27 completes the mat by making the illustrated stitches all over the mat where it is n t covered in black double wool.

No. 26.

No. 27.

After which, with a nice red fringe sewn round the border, and a lining at the back of coarse material, the mat is complete, and can be placed in front of the hearth or before a dressing-table.

Fig. 28.

Needle-Case.

An admirable invention for a needle-case, in which all the needles are threaded, has been sent me by a young lady, who has kindly permitted me to describe it here. It is on the principle of the rolled-up pocket needle-book; but inside the roll at the end are three reels of cotton, the ends of which are passed through the eyes of the needles, which are darned into the needle-book in three even rows. In this manner the needles are always fed by the cotton until the reels are empty, when the roll must be undone at the end and fresh reels supplied. It can be made of velvet or leather, or any material lined with flannel and bound with ribbon.

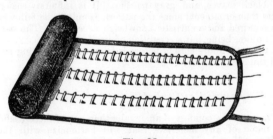

Fig. 29.

The annexed drawing will make this explanation clearer.

Embroidery is, at the date of this writing, the most popular of all kinds of work, both in dress and ornament, and it is a fortunate circumstance for many women that it is so, for hundreds have been kept in employment in the last two years, who would have starved had not the fashion of elaborate ornament on every article of dress been revived. And although machine embroidery has largely superseded that done by hand in cheaper goods, the finer work can never be rivalled, as no machine can follow the intricacies of design, or make the varied stitching required for really exquisite embroidered articles.

Most of the muslin embroidery is imported at so comparatively trifling a cost, that but few care to work any elaborate articles. But there is one branch of it that will always be popular. I mean Initial Embroidery, to do which well requires both care and skill, but which amply repays the worker for the time bestowed, since a handsomely embroidered initial is a handsome finish to every article of underwear, toilet muslin, and handkerchiefs, in the fair worker's possession.

The beautiful pillow shams, so much in fashion, are greatly improved by a large initial letter or monogram embroidered in the centre, and a bedroom can have no prettier addition to its elegance than initial lettering in embroidery upon pillow cases, sheets, towels, toilet mats and tidies, done in sets to match.

One of the most beautiful arts to be learned in connection with silk embroidery, is flower-drawing and painting. When a lady is proficient in this, she is independent of the pattern makers, and can present to her friends articles of beauty, not only embroidered, but designed by her own skill and taste.

In studying flower embroidery, make it the first object to become familiar with the peculiarities of form perceptible in every different class of flower. Not merely is the shape of each leaf and petal distinct, but the calyx, the bend of the branch, the mode of growth is characteristic in each separate species of flower. Irrespective of color, also an important consideration, this is imperative; for sketch correctly the merest outline of a rose-leaf, and it will not need color to distinguish it from a vine-leaf, while if the shape is incorrect, no coloring will make it appear perfect. Study the forms of the natural flowers until you can draw them accurately, and when you are competent to group them, and to rectify any errors in patterns you may buy, you will find the mere coloring a much simpler affair.

Embroidery proper is worked in colors similar to the articles copied, but this rule will not apply to dress, since variegated embroidery would be far too pronounced in effect for any but evening wear. Yet there is really something incongruous in brown roses, black leaves, and gray pansies. It is infinitely easier, therefore, to work for dress than ornament; since the pattern is only to be followed in one silk, no shading is required and no artistic knowledge necessary. The pattern is worked throughout alike, being but a repetition of itself.

But in articles of ornament, the more closely nature is followed in imitating her works the more beautiful the effect will be.

Invalid's Pocket.

Few things contribute more to the comfort of an invalid than one of these useful articles, which may be made of any materials that will harmonize with the furniture, but are most elegant if embroidered in the style of our specimen.

The materials are: half a yard of rich black satin; sarcenet, to correspond in color with the hangings; strong cardboard; wadding; pot-pourri; and nine yards of satin ribbon, the color of the lining.

Buy the satin nineteen and one-half inches wide, and divide it up the centre, having nine inches on one side, ten and one-half on the other. The narrower half forms the back, and leaves enough to make a small pincushion for one of the pockets. The other half forms the pockets.

These are three in number, the lowest having no division, the second one down the centre, the upper one two; so that there are really six pockets.

One group of flowers covers the lower pocket, two the centre; the third has an ornamental initial in the middle and a light spray on each side, and the divisions of the pockets are ornamented with a light pattern in embroidery. The little pincushion should also have some device worked on it.

The engraving will show the form of the whole complete article, as well as of the separate pockets.

To make it up: Cut a piece of cardboard, eight inches wide and about twelve long. Slope it, as in the pattern, and cover it with satin at the back, and wadded sarcenet on the other side.

Line each pocket with wadded sarcenet, scented with pot-pourri, and trim the top of each with the ribbon, quilted into a ruche.

Each pocket must be put on plain at the bottom, and sloped a little on each side, which the greater width will allow, so as to set rather full, and hold things conveniently.

Fig. 30.—INVALID'S POCKET.

When all are put on. the divisions must be made, and the whole trimmed with quilted ribbon.

These pockets are intended to hold watch, chain, and seals in the upper pocket; pincushion and smelling-bottle in the two centre; and the handkerchief in the lowest.

The embroidery to be done in fine floss. Similar watch-pockets may be done in canvas work.

Purse in Embroidery.

EMBROIDERED UPON STEEL-COLORED GLOVE-KID, IN HIGH COLORS.

The edges are trimmed with quilled ribbon, and the ends finished with silk to match. Cord and tassels of mixed silk to match the embroidery. The same design makes a handsome tobacco bag, when lined with oil-silk.

In conclusion, it must be remembered that every style of embroidery in any material depends entirely for its beauty upon the perfect evenness of the work. Irregularity of stitch is never intended to imply a straggling character of work, and roughness of surface must be always avoided. The outlines must be carefully drawn, distinctly defined, and then followed in working with the most exact accuracy.

Fig. 31.

Next in importance is the selection of good material. Embroidery being a luxury at best, it is better to do without it entirely than to have it upon inferior material or worked with poor wool or silk. In cotton embroidery it is best always to wash and iron the articles before the edges are cut, as the scallops have a firmer and more even appearance than when they are cut before washing. This, of course, does not apply to such work as can be worn before washing, but this should be carefully pressed before the edges are cut.

Embroidered Lamp-Screen, with Pattern of Work.

This screen is worked upon white crape in floss silk, the edges corded with coarse netting or crochet silk of the same color.

Under the dots and leaves are pieces

Fig. 33.—PATTERN OF WORK.

of contrasting silk, which show through the crape when the lamp is lighted, with beautiful effect. Green silk, with the work in golden brown, or cherry colored silk, with work in a deeper shade of red, is also effective.

Fig. 32.—EMBROIDERED LAMP-SCREEN.

CHAPTER II.

BRAIDING.

Braiding is generally considered the simplest of all the varieties of fancy work, and yet it requires some skill to make it handsome and durable. There was never probably a time when it was more fashionable than at present, for it is the stylish trimming for the most elaborate wraps and dresses now imported, and is universally used for linen dresses and every kind of clothing for children.

The imported sacques and wraps of every description, trimmed with elaborate braiding, and very expensive, may be imitated at home so perfectly that the difference can never be detected, at comparatively trifling cost, and the patterns can be stamped at the fancy stores upon any material required.

Cotton and Linen Braiding

is used for wash goods of all descriptions, being extremely fashionable for the linen and cambric dresses now worn, for underclothing, aprons and children's clothing. There are several kinds of braid to be procured.

French Plait Braid

is of various widths, determined by numbers. It comes in white, scarlet and mixed black and white, washes well, and has a firm, even edge.

Russia Braid

is not quite so fine, thicker, and gives a richer effect; it is used extensively for children's garments, and is the best for heavy material, such as Marseilles or pique.

Waved Braid

has a waved edge and requires great care in sewing it down, as each wave must be secured or it will wash into rolls and be extremely difficult to iron. This braid is also called Eugenie tape.

Alliance Braid,

a mixture of cotton and bright-colored worsted, is handsome and washes well. It is extensively used for children's garments, looking well upon natural-colored linen and on white and colored materials when in good contrast to the groundwork.

When the material has been selected and the braid chosen for working, the pattern must be traced very carefully, unless already stamped. It is cheaper to have the stamping done by experienced hands, but where this is impracticable, the pattern should be carefully traced upon tissue paper, basted down upon the material, carefully followed in thread in short, even stitches, and the paper torn away. The braid must be fastened upon the wrong side at the beginning of the work, carried through by being threaded in a coarse worsted-needle. The stitches should then be taken very close, across the braid, keeping the braid carefully on the lines forming the pattern, curving with very slight fulness and making points by sharply folding the braid over, if alike on both sides, or turning it sharply if not alike. The difficulty will be found to keep it from spreading at turns or curves. Broad braid must be run on both edges, and the patterns must have longer curves than are required for narrow braid.

The waved cotton braid is exceedingly pretty for aprons and children's wear, and it is very handsome for babies' linen or Marseilles cloaks, and for little girls' linen dresses. In making points, with either waved or plain braid, one stitch must always be taken across to secure th point, and broad braid must have a close running under the fold to keep the point in place.

Dresses

when braided, must be first sewed at every seam, that the pattern may not be uneven in crossing them. The basque or polonaise patterns come in all sizes, but unless a dress is fitted and basted before stamping, the effect is not good.

Wraps

of all descriptions must also be fitted and basted before stamping, to secure a handsome appearance.

Trimming

made by braiding a pattern upon a strip of the material of the dress or wrap, is far easier than braiding the actual garment, and is very much worn. It can be put on as a heading for ruffles or flounces, or made into ruffling or flouncing. In the latter case it must be always finished with a buttonhole-stitch scallop, in thread to match the braid.

Worsted and Silk Braid

are used for many ornamental purposes as well as for dress. The best known braids are

Plain Russian Braid,

so called from the threads being woven in what is known as Russian plait. Two plaits, the French and Russian, are used in braids, the latter having all the threads carried from the edge to the centre, insuring a very firm, even edge, highly desirable in working. It is very important in braiding to select braid that is close and firm, as it will wear far better than the loosely woven, and will not stretch so much in working.

Alliance Braid

comes in silk and wool, as well as in cotton, with the same variety, being of one color on one edge and a different color on the other. It is used principally for fancy dresses and ornamental articles. It can also be procured in gold or silver thread combined with colored silk, but is very expensive and wears black.

Star Braid

is a variety of waved braid with serrated edges. In worsted it washes well and is very pretty for children's aprons. In silk it is very effective in leaves and flowers. Besides the varieties mentioned, new braids are constantly being introduced into the market, to meet some caprice of fashion.

Braiding in Cord

comes under the same head as flat braiding, but is not done in the same manner. In selecting cord for braiding it is important to choose the softest and silkiest, as the stiff, hard cord will never curve into graceful patterns, and is very difficult to sew on. Lay the cord on the pattern, securing the end as the flat braid is secured. Holding it firmly, sew it down with stitches taken underneath, so as to be entirely invisible. Never cross the cord with stitches.

Chenille Braiding

is very difficult, requiring the greatest care to keep the material from roughening in the hands. Great skill is required to avoid injuring the pile. Use the finest silk procurable, and let it exactly cross the chenille, into which the needle must never go at all. Slip the needle under to the next stitch, and again cross it. The stitches should be about three to an inch. Hold both cord and chenille loosely, or the work will be likely to pucker.

Raised Braiding.

This effect is produced by sewing the braid down upon one edge only, if it is narrow; or if wide, by sewing it upon both edges, pushing them a little closer together than the actual width of the braid, so that it will stand up in relief. It is handsome, but difficult to work evenly, and does not wear well.

Gold and Silver Braiding

is much used for ornamental articles, for slippers, smoking caps, and cushions. The French braid is the best, wearing longer without tarnishing than any other. It should be sewed on with silk the exact color of the braid.

It is a good plan in sewing on silk and worsted braid to buy one piece more than is required for the work, cut it in yard lengths and draw out the threads to sew down the braid used to follow the pattern. In this way an exact match in color can be obtained.

Bead Braiding

is only difficult from the danger of crowding the beads, which will give the work a confused appearance. It is much in fashion for wraps, and is very handsome upon fine black cloth or black silk, worked in jet beads. These must be of the best quality, or they will cut through the silk. The lines marked for braiding must be carefully followed, putting on one bead at a time in a long back-stitch, bringing the needle out sufficiently ahead of the last bead to make room for the next one in the back-stitch. It may be done more rapidly but not so securely in another way. Secure the silk thread by a knot, and string the beads. Pass the thread along the pattern, and fasten it firmly at the other end. Secure the beads in place by a tiny stitch across the thread at every third bead. When bead braiding is done with gold beads, an edge of gold braid adds very much to the effect. Alternate rows of gold and steel beads have a very handsome effect on velvet.

Patterns in Turkish style, arabesque, key bordering, and other designs, are more effective for braiding than flowers or leaves, which are apt to look stiff. Grape leaves and steins in braid, however, with tendrils and grapes in silk embroidery, are very handsome for flannel work—infants' blankets and skirts especially.

When a child's dress is to be done in raised braiding, take care to select a pattern in which the lines never cross each other, which would at once destroy the effect.

A rather strong straw needle is the best for braiding in cord, but you cannot put on chenille or silk braid with too fine a needle. It should be long and thin.

If braid is sewed down with a sewing machine or carefully stitched on by hand, a line in the exact centre, of a contrasting color, is very effective.

All braiding requires to be pressed with a moderately cool iron when finished. Generally it may be done in the ordinary way, upon several folds of flannel, to ensure a very soft surface; but raised and chenille braiding must have the wrong side passed tightly over an iron held upright.

In making up embroidered or braided articles which are lined and wadded, it is a great finish to the whole to quilt the lining silk very neatly in small blocks or a pattern. It is very easy to do so. Take a piece of silk large enough to allow you to cut out the lining, fold it over and over, beginning with one corner; when it is all folded to look like one narrow strip, pass a cool iron along to crease it. Fold again in the contrary direction, and do the same. You may then cut it the proper shape, tack fine wadding under it, and run it in the creases, in fine stitches, or stitch it in the sewing machine with silk of contrasting color. Watch cases, pockets, glove cases and such articles, should be sprinkled with perfumed powder, on the wrong side, before being made up.

The calico case for the feathers of a soft cushion, should be cut crosswise and wadded before being filled with feathers or down. Down is the softest and will not so soon flatten. The wadding keeps the cushion in good shape longer than feathers or down alone.

Ribbon trimming must never be quilled too full; it spoils the effect.

Every knot of braid should be wound before using.

In all fancy work the greatest neatness is necessary in working and making up articles, as they will never pay for the labor bestowed if carelessly wrought or put together.

The Toilet Set.

PINCUSHION, GLOVE, AND HANDKERCHIEF CASES.

These are made of satin or velvet to correspond with each other, and with the bed-furniture and curtains. They are worked in silk braid of four different colors, one corner of each pattern being worked in a different color. The little centre pattern is worked in the same way, reversing the colors, and the whole braiding bordered with gold thread.

The pincushion is a card-board box, lined inside with wadded silk. The top is stuffed, to form a pincushion, and the sides are braided, each in a different color.

The glove and handkerchief cases are also lined with wadded silk, and scented.

Fig. 34.—THE TOILET SET.

and the whole are trimmed with cord or fringe to correspond, and are alike **pretty** and useful for a lady's dressing-room.

Toilet Mat.

The next pattern is designed for a toilet mat to match the set, and can be worked the full pattern for centre mat, and the centre pattern only for small cologne-bottle mats at each side.   They should be worked on fine white Marseilles, in colored cotton braid, to match the pincushion, glove, and handkerchief case.

A fringe can be added by buttonhole stitching cotton to match the braid, in long loop stitches.   They are very pretty worked in white star braid.

Fig. 35.—THE TOILET MAT.

CHAPTER III.

APPLIQUE WORK.

The term applique, or application work, applies to the style of embroidery in which a pattern is cut or stamped out of one kind of material, and transferred to another material, or the same in a different color, to which it is fastened by some edge of needlework, uniting by braid, satin stitch, cord or beads.

In white goods this style of work is called transfer work, and will be found under that heading, the term applique being generally confined to articles of cloth, velvet, satin or silk.

It is necessary in the first place to purchase a complete set of stamping tools, to secure accuracy of outline in patterns, stars, circles, or diamonds, but the patterns are procurable in all varieties already stamped out of velvet cloth, satin or silk.

When you have selected your pattern, baste it carefully down upon the material for your background, always having either fabric or color in contrast. Velvet on cloth, silk on velvet, cloth on silk—any combination most effective to the worker's eye, can be used. When carefully basted down, work the edge carefully in satin stitch, or run on a cord or braid, carefully covering the edge of the applique on both sides.

Many articles, such as slippers, sofa cushions, pincushions, smoking-caps and others, are very handsome done in velvet and cloth and finished with gold braid. A set pattern is more effective than leaves or flowers, although both are extensively used.

Patent Applique

is an easier form of the same work, and can be procured at all fancy stores. The pattern is stamped out upon the material but not cut through, the design being of a different color from the groundwork. The outlines must be braided or worked in satin stitch, exactly as in the genuine applique. The effect of this edge is to raise the inner work, so that it is impossible to tell that it is not actually laid on.

Many of the patterns are very elaborate, and there is a great gain in escaping the actual edge which will often escape from the most careful braiding, and soon wear ragged.

Cretonne Work.

This is a charming new style of application. The cretonne in every design and color can be procured at any fancy store, and the patterns must be cut out with very fine, sharp scissors. They are always clearly defined. Take a piece of the material—black satin being one of the favorite fabrics—suitable for a

Fig. 36.—FLORAL DESIGN

screen, cushion or any article chosen, and pin it down very firmly upon a
perfectly flat surface. Cut out your designs from the cretonne.

Birds are the most effective, being so brilliantly colored. Cut out a branch, say
apple-blossom, and such birds as you prefer. Lay these face downward, and
paste carefully with starch or very fine gum-arabic. Then lay them upon the
satin. It would be well first to place them on the satin, before starching or
gumming the back, to judge of the effect and mark the places where you wish
them to be with pins; then gum and attach them. It is then best to put the
work in a frame; but, if this is inconvenient, the cretonne must be further

Fig. 37.—BUTTERFLY DESIGN IN APPLIQUE.

attached by a stitch here and there, as it is liable to break away if much pulled.

Soft floss silk is the best for the cretonne edges, which must be very carefully
done. Care must be taken to make the down stitch always in the cretonne and
the up stitch in the satin, close to the cretonne margin. The edge must not be
made in overcasting, but in close fine satin stitch, blending with the coloring of the
cretonne.

When the cretonne designs are selected, the edge of each must be carefully
matched in every shade by the floss silk purchased. In the edges of birds and
flowers many colors and shades will be required, for each stitch must match as

closely as possible the painting of the edge it touches. When all the margins are worked, the labor of the undertaking is over, and its more tasteful phase begins. You must then work long stitches in the highest lights of every portion, using the lightest shades for this purpose, and in the dark parts use the very darkest shades; all this has to be done by a few long stitches, and the effect it produces is marvellous.

The middles of flowers should be worked in a knotting-stitch formed thus: Draw your needle out at the point where you wish to make the first knot; place the thumb of the left hand on the silk about an inch from where it emerges from the material, letting it stand in a loose loop; twist the needle in this from right to left till there are three coils on it; then put it over the thread near the thumb, and put the point firmly into the material, holding it with the left hand, while with the

Fig. 38. — CALLA LILY.

right you take the silk where the thumb of the left held it, and gently draw it tight; then hold the left thumb on the knot, while with the right hand you draw the needle through. A cluster of these knots makes a very effective centre to a flower. The stems, if fine, are very difficult to manage, because the cretonne is apt to give way; it is easier to cut them off and work the stems in embroidery. French cretonne is the best for this work; the heavy twilled cretonne is very difficult to manage, and the coloring is less delicate; the satin-faced has a fine effect, but is difficult to cut.

3

Table Bordering in Applique.

Take a piece of fine black cloth the length required. Cut circles in paper the size of a silver dollar, with a piece the size of a silver ten-cent piece cut out of the centre. Cut circles in colored llama cloth large enough to cover the paper ones. These are to be tacked down to the cloth with a piece of military braid, threaded through the circles as shown in illustration. They are then sewn on each edge to the cloth in buttonhole stitch with gold-colored embroidery silk. White beads are then sewn on the edge of circles and braid. The colored rings are to be put on in the following order: drab, crimson, blue, yellow, violet, green, pink, drab, crimson, and so in regular succession again. This makes a very handsome bordering for a table or mantelpiece, and the color of the material and rings may be varied to suit the taste of the worker.

Applique work combined with braiding and embroidery is very effective for

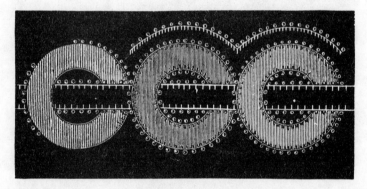

Fig. 39.—TABLE BORDERING.

cloth garments, but has become somewhat old-fashioned. With the revival of braiding and other trimming that passed out of date and again became fashionable, applique likewise is coming into favor. Some of the recent importations show it in two shades of one color upon street wraps.

It is a difficult fancy work, but for any purpose where velvet, cloth, satin, or silk is available, will be found to have the richest effect, well worth the trouble of conquering its difficulties.

A wall-pocket was recently shown the writer, of applique work in crimson velvet and black cloth, the edges in gold-colored satin stitch. The whole was mounted in black walnut, and was a very handsome ornament, intended for a library.

Applique Embroidery.

The foundation is of velvet. The design may be cut out of velvet or fine cloth, and is fastened to the foundation with cording-stitch in silk of two colors. The veins of the leaves are worked with fine silk.

Fig. 40.—DESIGN FOR CIGAR-CASE.

Lamp Mat in Applique Work.

The foundation is of velvet, with silk of three different shades of silk sewed on, as shown in illustration, with gold-colored silk braid, or gold braid.   Fringe of soft gold-colored silk laid in plaits at the top of scallops and points, having the effect of tassels.

Fig. 41.

CHAPTER IV.

CANVAS WORK.

Although there have been within the last few years many additions to canvas work both in material and in working, the general directions for the old-fashioned tapestry work will be found available for all of them, and will be given before each of the new kinds of canvas comes under consideration.

There are five kinds of stitches used in canvas work, although many more are sometimes reckoned; but these are but modifications and variations of the original five.

These stitches are: Cross Stitch, Tent Stitch, Tapestry Stitch—or Gobelin, German Stitch, Irish Stitch.

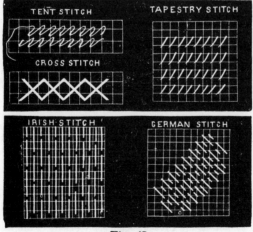

Fig. 42.

Cross Stitch

is worked by bringing up the needle on the left hand, then down on the right, upon the right again, and down on the left. This is reversed in all the other stitches, the needle being brought up in them on the right, and down on the left. Cross stitch is indeed a double stitch, being a stitch taken diagonally over two threads from left to right, and then a similar one being made from right to left, which, crossing the first, completes the stitch.

Tent Stitch

is worked by bringing the thread through the canvas on the right side, and down on the left, crossing over one thread each way. Four tent stitches thus occupy the space of one cross stitch.

Tapestry Stitch

is worked over two threads of canvas in height, and one in width ; in working a Berlin pattern, therefore, two stitches, side by side, are to be reckoned for every square, and it will then be of the same size as if worked in cross stitch, over which it has a great advantage in the supe.ior appearance of the shading, and the comparative fineness of the work. It is also the stitch the best adapted to work which is painted on the canvas, which should be embroidered in as artistic a manner as if a paint-brush were handled instead of a needle. Indeed, these painted canvas pictures should never be attempted by any one who has not some knowledge of painting, as the stitches cannot be counted, and it is very difficult to manage the shading with accuracy and smoothness. Persons ignorant of painting should obtain such patterns as are marked in blocks so as to be easily counted.

Irish Stitch

is very easy, and may be very rapidly done ; it is, therefore, very suitable for grounding. The first line of Irish stitch is worked by covering alternately two and four horizontal threads with the wool, leaving the perpendicular uncovered between ; in the second, and succeeding rows, the needle is brought up in the square where the wool had crossed only two threads, and crossing four horizontal threads is brought down ; it is then passed on to the next stitch of the short row. Reference to the engraving will show this to the learner.

German Stitch

is somewhat similar, but the stitches are diagonal, and alternately short and long throughout.

The canvas which forms the foundation of all Berlin work comes in great variety, many kinds being recently introduced into the market.

Cotton Canvas,

or French canvas, is the best for the ordinary work, such as slippers, chair covers, and other uses. All the threads are of the same color, firm, round, and square in the mesh. It is made in several degrees of fineness, which are determined by numbers.

German Canvas

is woven with every tenth thread of a different color, which makes it very easy to count ; but it is not so strong as the French, nor so true in the square, while the colored thread is apt to show through in light portions of the work. It will not bear stretching so well as the French, being more elastic in the web.

Penelope Canvas

is so-called from presenting the appearance of having been worked and the stitches picked out again. It is very nice for teaching children canvas work, as it is easily counted and does not strain the eyes. It requires double wool to fill the meshes.

Silk Canvas

does not require the work to be grounded. This is a great saving of labor, but it is not suitable for any article requiring much wear, being delicate and easily soiled. In the selection put the canvas over some dark material to ascertain if there are rough or uneven places in it. These spoil the appearance of the work, however carefully executed.

Rug Canvas

is one of the newer varieties, and comes in the natural color, a pretty shade of buff. It is coarse in web, requiring double zephyr to fill the meshes, but is very close, requiring no grounding. When worked in handsome patterns and heavily fringed, it makes a rug at once beautiful and serviceable. It is used also for carriage rugs, and other uses where heavy material is required.

Burlap Canvas

is a finer mesh of rug canvas, and much used for carriage rugs, chair covers, footstools, and other work where heavy material and the rich double zephyr are available.

Java Canvas

is extensively used for Berlin work that requires no grounding, and is very handsome worked in single or double zephyr, wears well but soils easily. It is very close in mesh, and firm in the web.

Panama Canvas

is a variety very largely used in combination with the straw that is so fashionable in many kinds of fancy work. It is a very stiff, harsh canvas, a pale, cuir color, matching the straw beautifully, needs no grounding, and makes its own fringe by ravelling the edges, and overcasting with a thread of the ravelling. It can be worked in any of the canvas stitches, and will contrast well either with the Berlin wool or with floss silk. Toilet-mats, card-baskets, and a great variety of small fancy articles, are manufactured of Panama canvas worked in floss silk and combined with straw in making them up. A very beautiful toilet-mat can be made by working a pattern in the centre of a small square of Panama canvas, fringing the edges about two inches deep, leaving six threads above the fringe and then drawing out six lengthwise. Fasten each edge of the fringe and heading with a buttonhole stitch between each crosswise thread, in silk to match the embroidered pattern. Line with bright-colored silk to the top of the fringe. It is easily made and very saleable at fairs, or suitable for a gift.

Net Canvas

comes in both black and white, is very strong and stiff, and will admit either of grounding or lining. It can be worked with double zephyr in cross stitch or filled with tapestry stitch. Mats made of the net canvas should have a fringe of wool on the edge ; run in the netting with a coarse needle, the mesh of the net forming the pattern as it crosses the wool. If grounded, it does not need lining, but is very pretty worked in a Berlin pattern and lined with bright-colored silk

The materials used for filling up canvas are wools of various kinds, called generally zephyrs, silks, and chenille. Beads are often used for grounding in pincushions and mats.

Berlin Wool

is emphatically the best used, being of superior finish, softer, smoother, and dyed in more lasting and brilliant colors than any other. For vaiiety and beauty of shading it stands unrivalled; and the peculiar weaving of the thread enables the worker to split it to any degree of fineness required, while for coarse work you can use it of two, or even three thicknesses. It comes, however, in three degrees of fineness, and one of these can generally be adapted to any work in hand. It is called the coarsest thread, double Berlin wool, medium thread, single, and finest split Berlin wool, or double, single, and split zephyr. It should never be wound for any work, and for canvas work should be cut into lengths and kept in shades.

English Wool

is rougher than the Berlin, but is a good foundation wool, wearing well. It does not come in such variety of color, but is good for coarser work or for children, being much cheaper than Berlin.

Germantown Wool

is a still cheaper zephyr, but inferior in color and quality to the imported goods. It is useful for sampler work for children, but not adapted to finer kinds of canvas work.

Fleecy Wool

is used more for tufted work on canvas than for flat stitches. It comes in all shades and colors.

Silk.

The kinds most used for canvas-work are floss, coarse and fine, Dacca, Berlin, crochet, and netting silk. Of these the floss, crochet and netting are used both in combination with wool and alone. With wool the floss silk for all the lightest shades of the various colors is very effective, adding greatly to the beauty of the work. And where gold is introduced into the pattern, hard-twisted crochet silk of gold color will be found quite as effective as the gold thread, and will keep its beauty much longer. Floss in gold color is not so good an imitation. Shaded silks in all colors are extensively used in canvas work, and as in embroidery, require accurate matching when a new thread is taken.

Chenille

for canvas work is much finer than that used for braiding, and is called embroidery chenille. It comes in all colors, and also in shaded colors, but requires great care in working, and is only suitable for articles that will not require frequent handling, as it soon wears rough. It is very delicate, and while catching the dust very easily, will not bear much brushing. At the same time, no work is so rich as that done in chenille. It must be used in short lengths, as it wears rough and thin in working, and in long threads makes the work appear uneven.

Needles.

Have both long and round-eyed needles ready for use, always selecting one amply large to carry the wool and silk and prevent it from fraying, yet not large enough to stretch the mesh of canvas through which it passes. For canvas alone, always use blunt points, but where the canvas is laid over other material, a sharp point must be used.

When doing very delicate work, use an ivory thimble, and if you find the warmth of your hands is running the colors of wool or silk, wash them in hot water and bran, drying very thoroughly before again touching the work. All canvas work should be done in a frame, and when the canvas is to be placed over other material for working through, allow it always a little larger every way, as most materials will be found to stretch more than the canvas in framing to work. The directions already given for framing the material for embroidery, apply as well to canvas work.

The next consideration in canvas work is the

Selection of Patterns,

which really demands great judgment and considerable artistic knowledge, if the effect produced by the work is in any way to compensate for the labor bestowed upon it and the expense incurred. A moment's glance at the patterns of the different kinds of canvas will show that the same design worked on each would have in every one a totally different appearance. But it requires further thought to prove that one style of design will advantageously bear to be worked smaller, and another kind will look larger than the original pattern. This point demands consideration and judgment.

The Berlin patterns, which are intended to represent historical, sacred, or other paintings, are mostly taken from the works of artists. Generally speaking, the originals are of considerably larger size than the Berlin pattern, and where this is the case you must calculate the stitches closely, as the work will probably greatly increase in size.

It is well when about to bestow upon work such labor and expense as are required to work these canvas pictures for framing, to see an engraved or painted copy of the original picture, and carefully note any difference. A careful comparison will probably give sufficient reason for this caution; for the Goths and Vandals who paint the Berlin patterns, not deeming the artists they copy sufficient judges of beauty and appropriateness to be implicitly followed, frequently think proper to add extraneous matters, with the same good sense and success, too, with which they would "gild refined gold, or paint the lily." Occasionally they err on the other side—cutting out some important figure or other accessory, which they, in their wisdom, deem superfluous.

Besides sacred and historical subjects, groups and wreaths of flowers may frequently be worked of an increased size with good effect. They should, however, be tolerably massive and compact, if worked more than one-third larger, as long stems, tendrils of vines, sweet peas or other straggling lines, would look stiff and clumsy, and altogether lose the graceful effect produced in smaller space.

When a pattern is to be worked on very fine canvas, the shades should be clearer and more distinct than in coarser material; care should be taken in working on silk canvas not to pass the thread from one part to another, as it will certainly show when completed.

Grounding

is the term applied to the filling in of the canvas after the subject is worked; generally this is done in one solid color, but occasionally in several shades of one color. This is the most difficult part of the work, as it must be perfectly even and smooth to look well. Very few workers upon canvas are proficients in grounding.

It should be executed with perfect regularity, and without the slightest appearance of lines. Begin at the lower left-hand corner, and work to the right, then back again to the left, crossing each stitch before beginning the next, if you are working in cross-stitch, and carefully making every upper stitch slant in one direction. To avoid joining always in one line, it is best to cut the wool for grounding in unequal lengths. Buy always an ample supply of wool for grounding before commencing it, as it may prove difficult to obtain an exact match, and the slightest difference will ruin the work.

Much time is saved by working on canvas over other materials, by which the labor of grounding is entirely dispensed with. It improves the appearance of such work, however, to purchase wool the exact color of the material, and fill in all spaces in the embroidery, and in finishing, work one stitch all round the pattern of the same color. This gives the work a richer raised look, and the canvas can be cut off close to the stitches, instead of being drawn out, thus securing greater richness of effect and a much smoother surface.

Colors Used in Grounding

must necessarily depend on the style of pattern to be worked; for the wools for the design and the grounding should always be selected with a view to harmony of color. The ground of a piece of work should always be a durable color; the dye should always be good, and not liable to rub off. Black, though effective, is not a good color for this purpose, as it wears rusty. Blue and lilac are apt to fade very soon, but rich, deep shades of dark colors, and very clear and brilliant shades of light, are the best. Drab, mode, gray, light brown, and stone in all shades, have a very cool effect. They wear well, but do not light up well in artificial light—either gas or candle. Some shades and colors are so delicate as to render it almost impossible to ground with them. Light blue is one of these; a good reason for always working in any sky tints in a landscape picture last, is that the sky would inevitably be of a hazy, muddy appearance instead of a bright blue, if a long piece of work was commenced by having the sky tints worked in first.

Never attempt a light ground on any but purest white canvas, as the effect will not be good.

Economy may be exercised in working by avoiding long stitches at the back, and the work will present also a more even appearance. Irish stitch or German stitch will look better in chenille than the closer stitches, and flowers, fruits, and birds are very handsome worked in this material.

Begin a centre piece always on the centre stitch; but all others at the lower left-hand corner.

Keep wools and silks in wash leather, excluded from the air. Silks and chenilles should be wound very lightly on card, and each card marked with the number of the shade.

Berlin wool should be cut in lengths and wrapped in long papers or calico, with the wool doubled over, to draw out at the loop.

Never mingle silk and wool in any work intended to imitate painting, as it ruins the effect.

The directions for beads on canvas will be found in the chapter on bead-work.

When patterns are drawn on the canvas they are more difficult to shade than those copied from a pattern with the defined stitch, and if it is necessary to repeat, it is better to copy exactly the first one worked, stitch for stitch.

Basket in Panama Canvas.

This basket is made upon Panama canvas embroidered in a Berlin wool **pattern.** It is made over cardboard and lined with quilted satin, and closes into the handle is shown in the engraving.

Fig. 43.

Fig. 44.

Shawl Strap in Canvas Work.

The pattern is worked upon canvas in bright-colored Berlin wool, and sewed down upon wide strips of leather, which is afterwards lined with silk, a crochet border knit all round, and made up as shown in illustration.

When canvas work is finished it should be taken from the frame and beaten carefully upon the wrong side until every particle of dust or loose thread is removed, but very gently, or the work will look dented. Prepare a table by laying out several thicknesses of woolen, covered first with white muslin, afterwards with canvas the same texture as that in the work. Over this, right side down, stretch the work, confining it with pins, to be perfectly even. Cover with a damp cloth (not wet) and press lightly and rapidly but thoroughly with a warm iron, not hot enough to injure delicate coloring.

Fig. 45.—SHAWL STRAP IN CANVAS WORK.

If the work is then to be put in a frame to hang, stretch it firmly over the sides, perfectly even, and fasten with very fine upholsterer's tacks.

Very elaborate pieces of canvas work for framing are not now in fashion, excepting for school girls, but every kind of smaller work is very popular, and at the end of this book, amongst the fancy articles described, will be found many that will require a knowledge of canvas work to execute. It is an accomplishment that dates back to remote ages, and which has never gone entirely out of use. The many new varieties of material in use at the present day, greatly reduce the labor of working, and simplify the designs, while the effect is as good, in many cases better, than the elaborate workmanship of those wonderful specimens of patience and skill handed down from our grandmothers.

Shopping Bag, in Canvas Work.

This pretty bag will be found most useful, and the sachels for shopping were never in more universal favor.

Materials—Canvas, No. 14, grey Berlin wool, coarse floss silks of a bright emerald green and gold color, gold thread, small pearl and garnet beads, white and gold tassels, cord, rings, half a yard of colored silk.

Work in any block pattern, and make up with silk lining, finishing with cord. The same work may be made up at an upholsterer's with a strong steel clasp, and will be more serviceable.

Fig. 46.—THE SHOPPING BAG.

CHAPTER V.

BEAD WORK.

Beads are now so generally used in trimming dress, as well as for strictly ornamental pieces of embroidery, that they seem to call for a separate chapter, although
it must be remembered that in every kind of embroidery, braiding, knitting, netting, crochet work, and canvas work, beads are always available.

All braiding patterns used in articles of dress that do not require washing, are
much enhanced in richness by adding beads, about six to an inch, either on one or
both edges of the braid, or in the centre. This is the simplest form of applying
beads to braiding patterns. It is still more effective to study the capabilities of a
pattern and apply the beads in masses. Thus, if a braiding or embroidery pattern represents acorns and oak leaves, let the inside of the acorn and of its cup be
filled in with beads, and all the veins in the leaves be thick with them. Black
velvet or cloth, with this pattern worked in floss silk and cut jet beads, is very rich,
and wears better than braiding alone. If a geometrical pattern is selected, let the
beads cluster heavily towards the centre of the design.

Lace, especially of the heavier kinds, is much improved by the addition of beads;
and here also the outline of the pattern must be followed, as the firmer work of
the lace is the best for attaching the beads. Each bead in lace work must be
sewed on separately, and in every kind of braiding and embroidery where beads
are introduced it will be found that attaching each bead separately, with a firm,
strong stitch, although tedious in execution, ensures greater beauty and durability.

Great care must be taken in selecting beads for articles of dress, as an edge that
is not perfectly smooth and round will cut the silk very soon, and require constant
renewing.

The introduction of beads in canvas work is very effective, and will always be
popular, because of its durability. A design well executed in beads alone is as
beautiful as a mosaic, and will last for a much longer time than if worked in silks
or wools. Black, dead white, or crystal beads, make a most beautiful grounding
for highly-colored designs in silk, wool or chenille, throwing out the colors in bold
relief.

A great variety of articles are embroidered entirely in colored beads, with good
effect, arabesque and scroll patterns being very beautiful in beads of one color
only, while flowers can be worked in shaded beads. The designs are the same as
those used in canvas work, and the stitch for canvas is always tent stitch.

The best thread for bead work upon canvas is a strongly-warped sewing-silk, or
firmly twisted cotton thread. In using colored beads, they should be carefully
sorted in small, shallow boxes, and taken from the box on the point of the needle.
Gold and silver beads especially, should never be handled.

It is difficult in this country to procure perfect shades in beads; but such as are required for white roses or lilies, can be obtained in any large fancy-work emporium, and also the shades of gold and brown. A group of flowers on geometrical pattern in these two sets of shades, grounded in the brilliant peacock blue now so extensively used, makes a beautiful design for a cushion, mat, foot-stool, or screen; it can be washed with flannel and fine white soap, when soiled, and with fair usage will last a hundred years, without loss of beauty. With a fringe of the same shades this work makes the most beautiful lambrequins for mantelpieces, tables and brackets.

All embroidery in beads, on any material, has a brilliant effect, and is suitable for most of the purposes to which silk and wool embroidery is applied. In gem patterns on canvas, beads can be introduced with wool, silk or chenille; and names or mottoes worked on embroidered cushions, satchels, glove-cases or other articles, in gold, steel or white beads, add greatly to the beauty of the design.

Steel beads are used for embroidering velvet, either black or colored, and have a very rich appearance, while steel bullion is effective with the beads for stems or tendrils. The pattern is to be traced as for all other embroidery, and the beads sewed on separately with waxed silk, as they are apt to cut. They must be laid on in such forms as the stitches would take if the pattern were worked in silks, or the character of the leaves and flowers will be lost.

A name or motto worked in beads may be set, as it were, in gold, by being entirely surrounded with gold braid, more or less fine. This has the effect of throwing the beads into strong relief.

Bugles are also extensively used in bead work, and come both in black and white. They are only available for articles of dress, being too long to work gracefully into any but line patterns for braiding.

When a piece of work entirely of beads is finished, it should be carefully stretched and held with pins upon a thick, soft surface, face downward. Then a solution of gum-arabic should be spread with a brush over the back, and left to dry. Three coats well dried between each application will make the work much more durable, as it holds the threads firmly in place, and lessens the danger of cutting. If the beads are of gold or steel, great care must be taken that the first coat of gum is not made too wet, as it will soak through and tarnish, but in glass or porcelain beads, if the right side should be wet, it can be polished with damp flannel afterwards.

A still more fashionable, but less enduring style of bead-work, is produced thus: Buy a yard of white cotton velvet, stretch it on a board, face downward, securing it firmly on the edges by pins set close together; cover the back with thick starch, applied with a pasting brush, taking great pains to keep a perfectly smooth, even surface. When quite dry, draw on the surface so starched the leaves, flowers, or other designs you wish to embroider upon the screen, cushion, or article you contemplate making. Have a piece of rich-colored velvet or cloth, suitable for the screen, ready. Cut out the designs in the white velvet by the lines you have drawn, and tack them on the colored material with very fine stitches in white thread. Then cover each leaf, flower or portion of the design with beads worked in very thickly, but not crowded. Crystal beads are the most effective for this purpose, as they glitter in artificial light with the brilliancy of tiny diamonds; and the introduction of a few steel beads for veining, and a few pearl-white ones for flower centres, makes a great improvement. A shade or two of green, crimson or brown, if they can be procured in transparent glass, may be introduced with good effect.

This style of bead work is very handsome for banner screens, hand screens, cushions, lamp mats, cologne stands, penwipers, and all light articles. Bead work is used for the separate pockets or bags that are in present fashion, in braiding patterns, and is very effective.

A style that is not new, but has never gone out of fashion, is the imitation of Indian work in dead-white beads upon cloth or flannel of a vivid scarlet, the edges finished by a bead fringe or scallops worked in white silk in buttonhole stitch. The pattern can be stamped upon the flannel or traced upon tissue paper, which can be basted down on the flannel, worked through and pulled away when the design is finished. To be a good imitation of the work done by the North American Indians, it must always be on scarlet material, worked in milk-white beads. A toilet set of pincushion, cushion mat, two cologne stands, and hanging watch-case, the patterns to match, is a very handsome bridal present.

Hanging-baskets in beads, although somewhat out of date, may still be seen. They are made by stringing large crystal beads upon strong but flexible wire, which is twisted into the required shape and fastened firmly with waxed crochet silk. The pendants are made by stringing the beads upon silk and fastening in loops. If for actual use they must be made over a wire frame that is strong enough to hold a glass dish to contain water for the flowers.

Bead book-marks are made by working names or mottoes in beads upon perforated card, and sewing them to a ribbon the width of the card.

Bead fringe, made by sewing beads to any piece of work in loops or ends, give a very handsome finish to pincushions and many fancy articles, and black silk fringe for dress use can be greatly improved by a narrow heading of black beads. We have seen a broad silk braid, stamped into a pattern, that was frayed and worn beyond all beauty, made into a rich trimming for a cashmere sacque, by the use of bead work. The braid was sewed in the usual manner upon the sacque, and then the stamped pattern was followed with jet beads sewed down separately, covering entirely the frayed satin surface, and leaving the heavier silk of the braid to still be seen as a groundwork. It had all the beauty of an imported wrap when finished. Old belt ribbons can be made very handsome again by tracing a pattern and covering it with beads, jet beads looking well upon any color.

Purses being once more in use for silver money, bead work can be largely introduced into their manufacture, both in knitting, crochet work, and embroidery. Handsome purses are made in fine glove kid of soft shades, embroidered in colored beads, and made up with steel clasps, or in velvet, embroidered in gold or steel beads with clasp to match. These are very fashionable, and all purses. whether knit or embroidered, are fastened with clasps, rings and tassels being entirely out of date.

In knitting or crochet work, with beads, all the beads to be used must be threaded upon the silk before the work is commenced. When a bead is wanted, it must be slipped on the thread to the stitch last taken and fastened by the next stitch.

In crochet work, to prevent the bead from slipping to the wrong side, bring the thread to the front on the first finger of the left hand; by keeping the bead in this way always in front, and putting the needle through the back loop of the next stitch, you can finish by drawing the thread through the back and make the last loop in the usual way.

There is a great difference in the quality of beads—glass, metal, and porcelain—and the best is the cheapest in the end. In purchasing, it is well to pass each string through the fingers, as inequalities may often be felt that are not easily seen. Bugles should be of one length, or, if used for canvas or silk embroidery, they will give all the work an uneven appearance.

The hole is another important consideration, as, if it is too fine, the thread used will not be of sufficient strength; if too large, the work will present an irregular appearance. The German beads are the best in quality and the most varied and brilliant in color.

For all black dress-wear the real jet bead will be found far handsomer, and more serviceable, than the glass ones, and less expensive in the end, though costing more at first. The work of embroidering in beads upon dress materials is so very tedious that it will never be found profitable to put it upon inferior goods or in inferior beads.

Pocket Embroidered in Beads.

The foundation is of black gros grain silk, and the embroidery of fine jet beads. If preferred, the material can match the dress with which the pocket is to be worn. The same design in cloth of vivid scarlet, worked in milk-white beads, makes a beautiful wall pocket.

Purse Embroidered in Beads.

The square is of canvas, embroidered in crystal beads, and grounded in Berlin wool. The border is of crystal and milk-white beads. The top is of silk to match the grounding.

Fig. 47.

Fig 48.

3

CHAPTER VI.

LACE WORK.

Lace, as we now know it, is not probably older than the end of the sixteenth century. Earlier fabrics of this kind, such as the "fine twined linen wrought with needlework," the "cauls" and "checker work" of the Old Testament, as well as the work mentioned by the ancient Greek and Roman authors, are evidently the produce of the needle only; not a woven texture, but embroidery, both colored and plain, together with an introduction of gold and silver thread. Doubtless among these early works there was an interlacing or knotting of threads as well as the sewed embroidery.

Sixteenth century cut work appears to be that which makes the nearest approach to modern point lace. "Cut work was made,' says a modern writer, "in several manners. The first consisted in arranging a network of threads upon a small frame, crossing and interlacing them into various complicated patterns. Beneath this network was gummed a piece of fine cloth called ' quintain,' from the town in Brittany where it was made. Then, with a needle, the network was sewn to the quintain by edging round those parts of the pattern that were to remain thick. The last operation was to cut away the superfluous cloth; hence the name of cut work. "Again, the pattern was made without any linen at all; threads, radiating at equal distances from one common centre, served as a framework to others, which were united to them in squares, triangles, rosettes and geometric forms worked over with buttonhole stitch—*point noue* forming in some parts open work, in others a heavy compact embroidery."

The knitting of lace is claimed by John Beckman, in his "History of Inventions, Discoveries, and Origins," to be a German invention. He writes:

"I will venture to assert that the knitting of lace is a German invention, first known about the middle of the sixteenth century; and I shall consider as true, until it be fully contradicted, the account given us that this art was found out before the year 1561, at St. Annaberg, by Barbara, wife of Christopher Uttman. This woman died in 1575, in the sixty-first year of her age, and that she was the inventress of this art is unanimously affirmed by all the annalists of that part of Saxony. About that period the mines were less productive, and the making of veils, an employment followed by the families of the miners, had declined, as there was little[7] demand for them. This new invention, therefore, was so much used that it was known in a short time among all the wives and daughters of the miners, and the lace which they manufactured, on account of the low price of labor, soon became fashionable, in opposition to the Italian lace, worked with the needle, and even supplanted it in commerce."

Italy appears to have been the cradle of the beautiful art of lace-making, and its earliest production a needle-made fabric. The celebrated Maria de Medicis is said to have introduced the use of lace into the French court from her native country; but to the sagacity of the famous Colbert, minister of Louis XIV , is due the credit of having established a manufactory of lace in France, by calling skilled work-women out of Italy, thence spreading itself into many of the French towns and villages.

The principal laces are Brussels, Mechlin, Valenciennes, Lisle, Chantilly, Alen-con, Spanish, Italian, Bedfordshire and Devonshire.

Brussels Lace

has always held a high position, and may be recognized by the great fineness of the ground, and by a peculiar rib surrounding the flowers and scrolls.

Mechlin Lace

is a very delicate, fine lace, with a small grounding or net, and flowers surrounded with a flat, silky looking thread.

Valenciennes Lace

is of excessive firmness, but wanting the border or cord around the design, as in Brussels or Mechlin. Some of the ornamental groundings of this lace are marvels of beauty and patient industry.

Lisle Lace

has a regular clear ground with quaint flowers, bordered as in Brussels.

Chantilly Lace

is usually black, and made with a silk thread. Blonde is also a silk lace, both black and white.

Point d'Alencon

is a lace of great richness and beauty, made entirely with the needle, and usually with a great subdivision of labor. The flowers and scrolls are delicately bordered.

Spanish and Venice Point Lace

have become familiar from the very successful imitations of these rich laces now manufactured, and the patterns given at the present day for enabling them to be made at home by any expert needlewoman.

Venice point, or rose point, as it is sometimes called, is a lace of great richness and beauty ; the design being formed of leaves, flowers and stems of a quaint, conventional form, projected in bold relief from the surface by an underpadding of thread, and ornamented with fillings in stitches of a curious and varied character.

Beyond these laces other towns and districts of Europe are celebrated for lace fabrics, but our space compels us now to turn our attention to the directions for the manufacture of lace work at home.

The first of these is :

Honiton Lace,

which may be divided into two kinds—applique and point ; the former includes all those laces which have the pattern applied and sewn to a net ground, originally all made on the pillow or with the needle, but in the present day, the pattern or sprigs are applied to machine-made net.

In making the Honiton applique it is best if possible to cut the thick work from

Fig. 49.—HONITON.

genuine Honiton lace and sew it down upon a fine Brussels net, in any handsome pattern. But the sprigs may be worked in crochet in precise imitation, and then be used. Directions will be found in the chapter on crochet work.

When the sprigs are finished, cut the exact shape of the article required in bright colored paper, allowing a margin of half an inch all round. On this tack the net, and then the edge, beginning always in the centre. Arrange the sprigs and tack them also in their places, using short stitches on the upper side, and long ones beneath. Sew all the sprigs on the net with very fine cotton. The net may be turned in on the right side and covered neatly with the edge and finished with a short close buttonhole stitch. Another imitation of Honiton is made by selecting a close pattern, working it in buttonhole stitch to meet at all points, upon cambric, and cutting away the cambric, filling the spaces with any of the stitches which will be described later in this chapter.

Point Honiton is made something in this way, having no net but meeting at every point of the sprigs and scrolls, and joined by threads wrought in any of the lace stitches.

Guipure Lace

is generally understood to mean that lace of which the pattern is formed by a continuous flat braid or tape, and is the easiest of all laces to imitate. The original is made on a pillow, but machine braids in perfect imitation can be pro-

Fig. 50.—GUIPURE.

cured at any fancy emporium. Large flowing scrolls and flowers of a peculiar form are the characteristics of guipure, while the fillings are very varied and sometimes a coarse geometrical grounding is introduced.

The great art in imitating this lace is to copy carefully the old, quaint forms of the original genuine lace, and the curious needlework fillings belonging to them.

Point Lace,

or, as tt is generally called, modern point lace, is a very fascinating employment for ladies—so many pretty and elegant articles can be made in it—and if worked with the great neatness and wonderful evenness of old point, there is no reason why it should not be as valuable. The materials required for this work are plain and fancy linen braids of the width suitable to the pattern to be worked; but many ladies prefer making their own braid, that the work may be entirely from their own hands.

It is scarcely advisable, however, as the home-made braid has rarely the evenness and finish of that procured at trifling cost.

Point Lace Butterfly.

It is better not to begin on too large a piece of work; we therefore give one of the butterflies so fashionable to wear now on colored ribbons in the hair, and which can always be put to some pretty use when that fashion is over.

Fig. 51.—BUTTERFLY.

There are six different stitches in it. Tack the braid very neatly on the outline of the butterfly, then fill in the stitches. Fill the upper part of the top wing thus: Fasten strands of thread across each way two at a time, as shown in the engraving; make the circle where the strands cross, passing the thread round two or three times; work over these threads two buttonhole stitches in the space between the two threads, three buttonhole stitches in the next space; repeat from first threads; twist your thread round the strand to the next crossing, and repeat till all the spaces are filled. Then the cobweb for the spots on the lower wing: fasten six strands firmly across the circle formed by the braid; take a fresh piece of thread and pass it round and round, under and over, leaving an end which will be in the middle. When the cobweb is the size shown in the engraving, pass the needle under it into the middle, then make one or two neat overcast stitches, which will fasten in the first end; then cut off both closely. In the division surrounding this cobweb work what is called spotted lace. This is worked backwards and forwards; work two buttonhole stitches close to one another, miss a space about the eighth of an inch, work two more buttonhole stitches close together, miss a space; repeat.   At the end of the row work two button-hole stitches down the side, and work back, the stitches to be worked into the space, and the space made over the stitches.   Work the remainder of the lower wing in honey-comb stitch.   Fasten the thread to the right-hand side of the work.

First row—Make long loops across, fastening to the braid with two close or buttonhole stitches at intervals of about a quarter of an inch apart.

Second row—Work twelve buttonhole stitches into each loop and one into the fastening.

Third row—The same as first, being careful to work the two close stitches into the centre of each loop.   To edge the butterfly, work all round the outline of it. Fasten the thread to the braid and work a buttonhole stitch, miss a small space, and leave about the same length of thread in the same place—about the eighth of an inch—and in some a quarter of an inch, according to the curve of it, but so that it will lie flat; when this is done, work into each loop of thread three button-hole stitches, pass the thread round a strong pin while the next stitch is worked; repeat the loop after every third stitch.   This completes the butterfly.

Point Lace Edging.

The same stitches described for working the butterfly can be used to make the edging, of which the engraving gives the best suggestion to the worker.

Fig. 52.—POINT LACE EDGING.

A few of the most desirable stitches are the

Spider's Web Stitch.

Fig. 53.—SPIDER'S WEB.

This is worked with a fine thread and requires a very sharp needle. Fasten a number of strands across—according to the space to be filled—sixteen or twenty; twist each strand back as you make it; when you come to the last—twist back to the centre only—run the thread three or four times under and over the alternate strands, then twist once down the last strand, and carry the thread round, passing the needle through each strand, and, if possible, splitting the thread; continue till the space is filled. For all round spaces this stitch is the most desirable and effective, but requires practice to make it perfectly even, and looks badly if irregular.

Borghese Point Stitch.

The Borghese stitch is much used in the old Roman point, and the most effective stitch known. The stitch is always worked from right to left, and is button-

Fig. 54.

hole stitch, with a double twist, the thread being twisted back from the end of the row by passing the needle up between each stitch, and twice or three times in a space according to the length. To avoid repetition, the twist back, from left to right, is to be done after every row, and will not be mentioned again, but will be understood, and in the description each row will begin from the right-hand side.

First row: Work six stitches, miss the space of five; repeat.

Second row: Work five stitches over the six, and six stitches into the space of the five.

Third row: Miss five and work six stitches.

Fourth row: Work six stitches into the loop, and five over the six; repeat.

Another Borghese point is made thus:

First row: Work two stitches, the same as in the preceding directions miss the space of two; repeat.

Second row: Work two stitches into the space; miss two, repeat, and so proceed in alternate rows.

Point de Louvaine.

Fig. 55.

Fasten strands across the work at distances of rather more than quarter of an inch, as shown in the engraving; then fasten a perpendicular strand; twist down this to the first horizontal one, and work as follows: Make a stitch at second strand; bring the thread over first strand and make a stitch at third strand, then back to first strand; repeat, keeping the threads that pass over first strand very even.

Delecarlian Stitch

is a grounding stitch, worked from right to left. Insert the needle in the braid, bring it down in a simple sewing stitch, leaving it a little loose; then pass the needle over the thread, going up to the braid; under the thread, coming down.

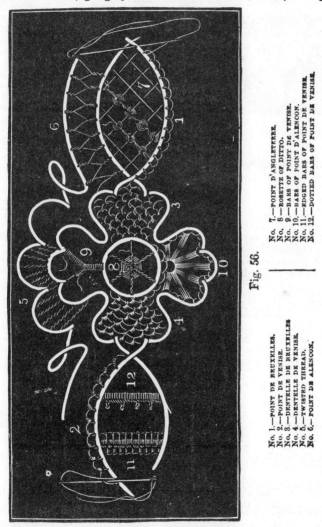

Fig. 56.

No. 1.—POINT DE BRUXELLES.
No. 2.—POINT DE VENISE.
No. 3.—DENTELLE DE BRUXELLES
No. 4.—DENTELLE DE VENISE.
No. 5.—TWISTED THREAD.
No. 6.—POINT DE ALENCON.

No. 7.—POINT D'ANGLETERRE.
No. 8—ROSETTE OF DITTO.
No. 9.—BARS OF POINT DE VENISE.
No. 10.—BARS OF POINT D'ALENCON.
No. 11.—EDGED BARS OF POINT DE VENISE
No. 12.—DOTTED BARS OF POINT DE VENISE.

Draw tight when the row is finished. Twist the thread back, and proceed as before, being careful to keep the squares as even as possible.

The chart of stitches here given will aid in the description of twelve more bea٥ tiful stitches for the production of modern Point lace, and should be carefully studied before working.

Point de Colbert.

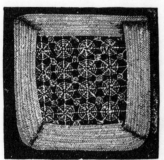

Fig. 57.

This is a very beautiful stitch, and is suitable either as a grounding stitch or for filling spaces large enough to show the beauty of the design.

Fasten straight strands across each way, about a quarter of an inch apart; then fasten diag٥na strands each way; where they all join, run the thread round twice, under and over the strands alternately; then work with a sort of back stitch, passing the needle under two strands, then taking it over the last of these two, under the same, and one beyond; repeat. Work five or six rounds in this way, according to the size you wish the star to be; make a little dot in the centre of the square by running the thread round three times.

Point de Bruxelles.

This stitch is simply the ordinary buttonhole stitch, which is worked on the edge of the braid, but not so close to it that the work will be liable to fray. The stitches are not to be taken close together, but about fourteen to the inch. This stitch must be worked from left to right, and the thread must not be drawn tightly, but must form a small loop, as in the engraving. Generally the entire edge of the braid must be worked in Point de Bruxelles or Point de Venise.

Point de Venise

is a heavier and handsomer edging than the Point de Bruxelles. It looks better, therefore, than that stitch, for the outer edge of collars, cuffs, and other articles.

Work a stitch of Point de Bruxelles on the braid, and in the loop thus formed 'work four tight stitches, passing the needle under the loop and the thread which comes from the braid, and over the remaining part of the thread.

Dentelle de Bruxelles

is made by filling up a given space of lines of Point de Bruxelles, working them alternately from left to right, and from right to left. In making Dentelle de Bruxelles and de Venise the needle is put through the loop of the preceding line, to form tle second and following lines; and in working the last one, the needle must be caught in the braid after every stitch, to attach it properly.

Dentelle de Venise

is formed by working a number of rows of Point de Venise, to fill up a leaf, flower or section of either. As this stitch must always be worked from left to right, it is imperative to either fasten off at the end of every line or slip the thread round to the place where the next line is to begin. In working alternate rows of Point de

Bruxelles and Point de Venise, the Point de Venise is worked from left to right, the other from right to left; and the needle must be passed through the braid at the end of every row.

A more simple edging than the Point de Venise, and more elaborate than Point de Bruxelles, is made by working one tight stitch in every loop; it is called Petit Point de Venise.

Twisted Thread.

This is worked by taking a stitch across an open space, and then another back to the same place, twisting the second thread several times round the first. It is impossible to say how many times the twist should be made, as it depends wholly upon the size of the space to be filled. If the open part be an inch in diameter, twist the thread seven or eight times, and in other spaces proportionately, more or less.

Point d'Alencon

is merely the old-fashioned herring-bone stitch, with a twist after it, formed by passing the needle under the thread of the last stitch before making another. It is used to connect lines of Point de Venise or Point de Bruxelles, or sometimes to join the edges of braid.

Point d'Angleterre.

This stitch is chiefly used to fill up large spaces, such as the principal divisions of a rose, or other open part. It is made thus: Make a series of bars across the part to be filled up, at distances of about the eighth of an inch apart, making every separate line firm by taking one or two stitches in the braid to secure it. When all the bars are made in one direction, cross them with others, at the same distance apart, taking care to slip the needle alternately under and over the threads so crossed.

At every place where the bars cross each other a small spot is to be worked, by passing the thread five or six times round it, alternately over and under the bar. Twist the thread twice round the thread to bring your needle to the next cross, which you will work in the same manner.

Rosette of Point d'Angleterre

is a single large spot, sometimes used to fill up a vacant space. The space is crossed with four or six twisted threads, the cotton being run through the braid from one point to another. The last single bar is only to be twisted to the centre, where they all meet. Work a stitch of Point de Bruxelles to connect them together, and work all round the centre by passing the needle round one thread and under the second; round the second and under the third; round the third and under the fourth, and so on. Work as many rounds as the size of the space may suggest, remembering it is not intended the rosette should fill up the space, in which it is merely to form a heavy spot. The last round must be worked only as far as the single thread, on which the thread must be twisted and fastened off.

Bars of Point de Venise

are merely bars of buttonhole stitch worked on two or three threads passed from one line of braid to another. Sometimes these bars are made to take the form of a cross; thus, having worked half the length of the bar in buttonhole stitch, make a bar at right angles with it, and work that down; then another in the opposite direction, and finally finish the first bar. Sometimes these bars are edged with Point de Bruxelles or Petit Point de Venise.

Bars of Point d'Alencon.

These bars are used to connect two lines of Point de Bruxelles or Point de Venise. Begin by putting the needle through a stitch, bringing it out underneath it; then through one in the opposite line; back into the first Venise or Bruxelles

Fig. 58.—INFANT'S DRESS, IN POINT LACE WAIST, SLEEVES AND BAND.

stitch, and again into the same opposite one. Do this three or four times. Then, missing one stitch, make another bar on the second, and so on.

To give these bars a good effect in some places, it is necessary to miss more stitches on one line than on the other.   For instance, if a semi-circular space were to be so filled, two stitches at least should be missed in the larger half of the circle, where one would be left in the smaller, as the bars should radiate from a common centre.

Edged Bars in Point de Venise.

These are simply bars of Point de Venise, edged with Petit Point de Venise. They are frequently used for the centre fibres of leaves and other similar parts.

Dotted Bars of Point de Venise.

Work the thread across the space from right to left, and on the bars thus formed make four or five stitches of Point de Bruxelles ; instead of drawing the last thread tight, make it long, by putting a needle in it to form a loop.   Work three stitches in this, then more on the bar, and repeat.

The next bar may be passed through the points of the spots thus formed.

Infant's Dress in Point Lace.

WAIST, SLEEVES AND BAND.

This pattern combines the two kinds of work ; the daisies which are grouped in the different parts being formed in tatting, while the rest of the work is done in the point-lace stitches.

The daisies are somewhat small, and have only three picots each.   Fourteen are required for the waist, and six for each sleeve.   The number necessary for the insertion depends, of course, on its length ; they are alternated with the leaves.

The leaves are worked round in Point de Venise, the inside and the rest of the braid in Point de Bruxelles.   All the leaves in the waist are worked uniformly, with a bar of Point de Venise in the centre, the intermediate spaces being filled with Point d'Alencon.   In the sleeves the leaves are filled with Point d'Angleterre, and in the band they are done alternately like those in the waist, and with Dentelle de Bruxelles.

All the points are connected together throughout with Point d'Alencon.

Two Handkerchief Corners.

In working the handkerchief, Fig. 59, right pattern, three pieces of braid will be required, as there are three distinct lines, which constantly cross each other. It is advisable not to begin putting on all the lines of braid in the same place, as the joins might then be more visible than they ought to be.   The engraved patterns give only one quarter of each handkerchief, which must be braided, and completely worked ; the stitches at the back are then cut, the pattern re-arranged, the braiding continued, filled up, and again taken from the paper; the process being continued until the whole is completed.

To keep the braid disentangled, each piece should be wound on a small card, and when the braiding for the quarter of the handkerchief is done, the cards should be put in a small silk bag, attached to the paper pattern.

The outer edge is worked in Point de Venise, as are also the outer line of the heart in the centre of the side, and some parts of the corner.   The rest of the braid is edged with Point de Bruxelles, excepting the wheels, which are left unedged.

The heart is filled up with Point d'Angleterre, worked rather closely, and with small spots; the outer part in the same stitch, but with larger spots, on lines placed at greater distances.

Fig. 59.—TWO HANDKERCHIEF BORDERS.

The wheels, of which there are three between the heart and the corner, that is, six on each side of the handkerchief, consist of three circles, one within the other.

The largest is worked in Dentelle de Bruxelles, and the second in Point d'Alencon ; in the centre of the third, or inner circle, is worked a rosette of Point d'Angleterre on eight threads, which divide the circle into as many compartments; every alternate compartment is then filled up with Point d'Angleterre. Some part of the corner is filled up with the same stitch, as is also the division where the initial is formed in braid ; but the greater part of the border, near the inner edge, is worked in Dentelle de Bruxelles.

Handkerchief, No. 2.

This pattern, left hand in Fig. 59, like the preceding, contains three distinct lines of braiding, namely, one which is to unite the border to the cambric, and two for the pattern. These last cross each other continually, the line which forms the Vandyke of one point making the centre of the next, and *vice versa.*

The edge is worked in Point de Venise, as is also that part of the braid nearest the inner line ; the other side of all the braid of the Vandyke, as well as both sides of the circle, being edged with Point de Bruxelles. In each circle is a rosette of Point d'Angleterre, worked not less than eleven times round, and the space between the circle and the point is filled up by radiating bars of Point d'Alencon. The corner is filled up with Point d'Angleterre, worked somewhat closely ; and a single spot of the same stitch fills up each of the small rounds made in the braid near the inner line.

One edge of the inner line of braid is worked in Point de Bruxelles, and this is connected with the rest of the pattern by Point d'Alencon.

This pattern, with a corner, is a handkerchief border ; but it is also suitable as an edging to trim a dress, or anything else, for which you would use point lace.

Not the least remarkable feature in the tastes of the present day is the rage for old lace, which has revived after the lapse of many years, during which comparatively paltry and inexpensive laces have been worn. There can be no question that the heavy and elaborate point lace is incomparably superior in effect to the loom manufactures which for so many years superseded it, but its expense places it beyond the reach of the majority, and therefore the directions for making it have been given elaborately that the readers of this little book may possess the art of reproducing the beautiful fabric by their own skill.

Even the most trifling articles in point lace are at present luxuries which only the wealthy can possess,. For this there are two causes. It is true that point lace, being done entirely by hand, will always be more expensive, as well as more durable, than any machine-made article can be, but the great scarcity of real point lace is the great cause of the extravagant price paid for it.

In former times it was the employment of the inmates of religious houses, the monotony of whose existence was diversified by the production of those exquisite pieces of needlework now regarded as precious treasures by their possessors. Now young ladies do not require to be immured within convent walls whilst acquiring any beautiful art, but it is greatly to be desired that they should perfect themselves in the delicate employment only suited to dainty fingers and requiring taste and exquisite neatness. No art can be easier to acquire than that of making point lace, and certainly no ornamental needlework can be more exquisitely beautiful when done.

Another style of lace-work, differing from those already described, is made upon net or cambric, and was formerly classed under the head of Bobbinet. In this, as in everything else, fashion's caprices can never be depended upon, and it is dropped and revived like other fancy work.

The material for the foundation of this work may be very sheer fine lawn, fine Brussels net, or Swiss muslin, very fine. The patterns generally are small and delicate, and the designs are governed by the article to be made. Every style of neck-wear can be made in this style of lace-work at comparatively trifling cost.

The pattern must be carefully drawn on paper and the lawn or muslin laid over it, and the design carefully marked with a fine camel's hair brush dipped in a mixture of thin gum water and indigo, unless it can be stamped at a fancy store, which is always preferable.

The pattern being drawn, the net is next carefully basted upon the wrong side. The pattern must be then run on in fine embroidery cotton, and worked over in the same, the stitch being governed by the character of the pattern; edges being done in buttonhole stitch, leaves or flowers in satin stitch, and stems in over stitch. When a good design has been selected, and is well and neatly worked, this kind of lace has a very rich effect. When the work is finished, the embroidered places must be carefully fastened in very close fine stitches at the edge, after which the lawn must be cut away, leaving the net for a groundwork.

Handkerchief squares must be made of fine linen lawn, buttonhole stitched on the edge, and the corners worked as described, the net, after the lawn is cut away, being carefully fastened down along the edge of the embroidery, on the wrong side. They can be stamped or marked in monogram or initial in one corner, the other three in a pretty pattern, and all embroidered in lace-work.

Another kind of lace-work is done with cotton upon net alone, and a coarser kind is often very effective in split Berlin wool upon colored net. It has the net worked over in spots, sprigs, or buttonhole stitch scollops or points, not taking the stitches too close.

A very elegant scarf or necktie may be made in this kind of lace-work by working black or white blonde in colored floss silk. The pattern for the edges should be narrow and the ends deep.

A thousand pretty things can be made in this work, rapidly done and inexpensive. Covers made of white net and cotton, with a simple pattern, put over soiled pincushions or other articles of silk or satin, will make them appear almost new again.

CHAPTER VII.

TATTING.

If any old Point Lace is carefully examined, there will frequently be found attached to it an edging of loops, made in a kind of buttonhole stitch, sometimes ornamented with very tiny points, almost resembling those in pearl edging; lines of the same material, similarly spotted, are used also to connect the more solid parts on the same work.

These loops and lines, looking like buttonhole stitch, are made with a small instrument called a SHUTTLE, of which there is a representation in the engraving, and the art of making them is termed the art of tatting or frivolite.

After dying out, as all fancy work will do at times, the art of tatting has been lately revived, and some of the most beautiful work imaginable in this form was exhibited at the Centennial International Exhibition in Philadelphia. One piece of work, a bureau cover, in rosettes of tatting, in No. 200 spool-cotton, placed over rose-colored satin, to display its fineness, was universally taken for the finest thread lace, and was as delicate as a spider's web.

It is a very strong and serviceable edge for underclothing of all kinds, for children's aprons and other garments requiring frequent washing, and can be made very rapidly and without any strain upon the eyesight.

The implements required for tatting will be more readily understood by reference to the engraving. Figure six is the shuttle, figure seven a pin attached by a chain to a ring. The pin is used in forming the pearling, or picot, as the French call it, and when pearled tatting is done, the ring must be slipped on the thumb of the left hand, and thus the pin will always be ready for use.

The cotton used for tatting is soft, and not too closely twisted. Thread that is much twisted is very apt to knot, which makes it exceedingly difficult to work. Very pretty trimming may be made of tatting in silk, of a color to suit the garment for which it is intended. The silk to be used is the fine or coarse netting silk, in selecting which great taste may be exercised. Two different sizes of the same shade, or even two colors may be united in the same trimming, with good effect, as, for instance, in the third pattern in the engraving, where the large loop might be made of a coarse black, and the surrounding loops of a fine, bright-colored silk, forming a beautiful trimming for a child's sacque or an opera flannel breakfast sacque. The silk will be found much easier to manage in tatting than any cotton that can be used.

The first consideration in tatting is the mode of holding the hands.

5

Hold the shuttle between the thumb and the first and second fingers of the right hand, and the thread within two or three inches of the end, between the thumb

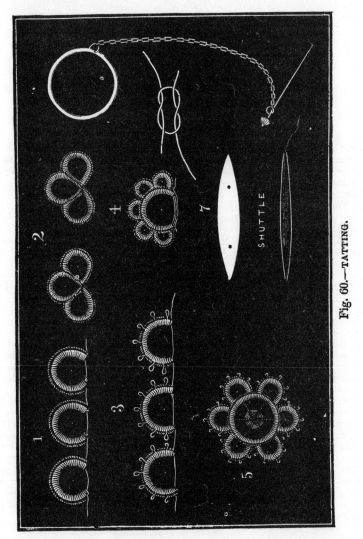

Fig. 60.—TATTING.

and first finger of the left hand, letting the end fall in the palm of the hand; with the right hand carry the thread round all the fingers cf the left hand, they being kept rather apart from each other, and bring the thread again between the thumb and first finger, where it must be held, thus forming a circle round the fingers. Having placed your hands in this position, you are ready to begin working.

There are only two stitches used in tatting, namely, the English and the French stitches; either may be used separately, but as the prettiest edge is formed by using both alternately, I shall, in these directions, use the term double stitch, to signify one of each.

English Stitch.

Having placed the hands as described, let the thread which passes from between the first finger and thumb of the left hand, and the shuttle, fall towards you; slip the shuttle under the loop between the first and second fingers, and draw it out towards the right, in a horizontal position, when a loop will be found on it, with the thread which was passed round the fingers of the left hand. Hold the shuttle steadily in the same position, with the thread attached, tightly stretched, and with the second finger of the left hand work the loop up to the first finger and thumb, when the hands will have resumed the first position.

Observe that the knot is always formed by the thread which passes round the fingers of the left hand; if this is not done, the loop will not draw up.

French Stitch

is made like English stitch, except that instead of allowing the thread to fall towards you, and passing the shuttle downwards, you throw the thread in a sort of loop over the left hand and pass the shuttle under the thread, between the first and second fingers, upwards.

Pearl Edging.

After making a given number of stitches, twist the pin in the thread, and continue working, holding the pin between the thumb and first finger; repeat the process, with as many single or double stitches between as you may desire.

Tatting possesses one great advantage—it can be worked in the smallest pieces that may be desired. They are united, when attached to the work they are intended to ornament, simply by laying the ends of the threads that are left along the work, and sewing them, so that the loops come into their proper places.

Pieces of tatting should never be knotted together, as it is very difficult to unite them quite closely; and, besides, knots are clumsy and bungling things to conceal in any sewing. Keep an envelope in your pocket, and if your thread breaks or gets soiled, cut off the piece you have finished at once, leaving an inch of thread, and put it away. If you make a loop which will not draw up, cut the thread and unpick it.

To do tatting well requires a cool, dry hand. In the engraving you will find five varieties of tatting, all of which are perfectly simple and easy to make.

Fig. 1 is the common tatting edge, made of a given number of double stitches,, from twenty to thirty, drawn into a loop.

Fig. 2 is called the

Shamrock Stitch.

It is formed thus: Make three loops of tatting, drawing up each quite tight, and leaving a little space on the cotton before making the next three. Each set must then be united in the form of a shamrock or trefoil, with a needle and fine thread; and in forming a border of them, place them in the position shown in the engraving, making them touch each other.

Fig. 3 is the common tatting loop with the pearled edge, and the mode of working it has been already described. The shamrock may be made also with a single edge.

Fig. 4 is a very pretty variety of the common edging. A large loop being made, five small ones are made close to it, and drawn up sufficiently tight to go round the outer edge of the large loop, round which they are afterwards to be sewed. An inch or two of cotton should be left, before the next large loop is made. This may be called the

Hen and Chickens Pattern.

Fig. 5 is made partly in tatting and partly in one of the point lace stitches. The circle being made, and the small loops sewed securely to the edge, the centre is filled thus : draw three strands of thread across to meet in the centre of the space inside the circle. Fasten a thread securely to the centre, connecting the threads firmly, and work out on each line in Point de Venise, passing the thread from the edge back to the centre for each one. In the middle, work the spot by passing the thread alternately under and over the bars in circles.

The Weaver's Knot.

Fig. 8 is used for securely fastening wool of cotton.

There is a great variety of edging to be made by varying the loops, and wider handsome borders are made by making successions of stars, first three, then two and then one, forming a point, and carried along the edge of the article to be trimmed.

A lambrequin of tatting in green Berlin wool, with this six-star point, every loop pearled in gold-colored saddler's silk, was one of the most beautiful specimens of tatting I have ever seen. It ornamented a round table covered with green cloth embroidered in gold color. This cover was tacked to the edge of the table, and the lambrequin of tatting sewed on the edge, making a very handsome article of furniture out of a table scratched to shabbiness on the top by constant use.

Child's Dress.

The following engraving gives the pattern for a child's dress trimming done in tatting and point lace stitches combined. It is worked upon a foundation of fine Swiss muslin, on which the pattern is traced in braid, the flowers and leaves worked in the stitches described in chapter on point lace, the muslin being left to connect them together.

This style of work is done more rapidly than the point lace work proper, and has the advantage of being close, and therefore more suitable for children's wear.

The muslin must not be cut away from the open parts until the whole is completely finished; and to prevent the muslin from tearing, the edges of point must be worked very close and firm.

The engraving represents the waist-sleeve, insertion and edging for the dress. The insertion may be used either for the band, or as an ornamental finish to the hem and tucks of a little girl's dress, for which purpose I should recommend its being worked on the muslin, without the two straight lines of braid, which now form the border; it will then have a less stiff and formal appearance than it has at present.

Fig. 61.—CHILD'S DRESS.

As it requires very nearly the full breadth of mull-muslin to make the body of child's dress sufficiently full, tear off a width, of a depth suited to the age of the child, and having tacked the pattern in the centre work on it, leave the two ends for the remainder of the body.

The pattern of the waist contains a complete centre-piece, unconnected with any other part; the two lines which form the top are done with another piece of braid, and all the remaining parts of the pattern are traced in one continuous line.

The middle group consists of a centre flower, with one on each side of it. The upper part of the former is filled with dentelle de Bruxelles, all the other parts being united by point d'Alencon. The upper part of the large flowers of the centre has a bar of point de Venise, edged with point de Bruxelles in the middle, and is united on each side by bars of point d'Alencon; point d'Angleterre fills up the middle, and radiating bars of point d'Alencon, the lower division of these flowers, all the narrow points being connected by point d'Alencon. This stitch also unites the two straight lines at the top of the stomacher. The open space between the second and third lines is filled with diagonal bars of point d'Alencon, with one perpendicular in the centre.

The remaining leaves and the roses are filled in dentelle de Bruxelles, and the lilies in radiating bars of point d'Alencon.

The sleeve must be worked to correspond with the stomacher, and a glance at the engraving will at once show in what stitches the insertion is to be worked.

The edging is of tatting. The loops, as you will perceive, are of unequal sizes, being alternately large and small. Make a loop of 24 double stitches, draw it up, and then make one of 20, with a *picot* or *pearl-stitch* after every fifth but the last; draw this loop up, and make one of 30, with picots as before, and then another of 20. These three picoted loops must be so drawn up that they will just go round the first. In the next set of loops, the first is to be made of 32 double stitches, with 3 picoted, all the same size, round.

When they are sewed on, they must be placed close together.

Case for Tatting Implements.

This beautiful case is made of fine French kid, of any neutral tint, embroidered in tatting, in crochet-silk of bright colors, and lined with silk to match.

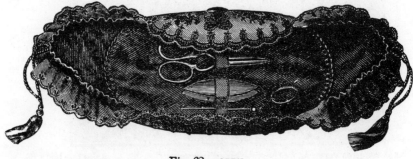

Fig. 62.—OPEN.

Fig. 63.—CLOSED.

End for a Necktie.

To be made in tatting of fine cotton, and sewed neatly to a tie or bow of fine Brussels net.

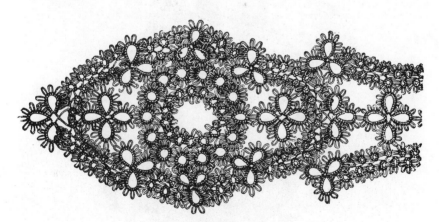

Fig. 64.

Wall Pincushion.

This pincushion is made of colored satin, with broad ribbons to match.   The tatting is in crochet-silk of a contrasting color.

Fig. 65.

CHAPTER VIII.

KNITTING.

Knitting is an art of comparatively modern invention. The honor of origin is disputed, but it is generally attributed to the Spaniards or Italians, as they attained great proficiency in the art before it was known to any extent in other countries. The Scotch, however, lay claim also to the invention, but although now very expert knitters, they have not succeeded in proving their claim.

A knowledge of knitting has so many advantages that it is almost superfluous to enumerate them. Little girls can knit wash-rags, stockings for the baby, scarfs and other simple articles; young ladies can knit so many beautiful pieces of fancy work that their mere names would fill a volume; socks for papa, breakfast shawls for mamma, hoods for grandma, scarfs and pulse warmers for grandpa, clouds for each other, and a variety of ornamental and useful gifts for holiday times.

The importance of knitting can hardly be over-estimated, as no machine work has yet reached the perfection of hand-knit articles. Knitting is really the employment of the million, rich and poor, old and young, gentle and simple resorting to it for amusement or occupation.

And for this there is excellent reason. The cheapness of materials required, the simplicity of the work, the scope it affords for the exercise of taste and ingenuity, and the very small amount of attention and application it requires, have placed the art within the reach of the most humble, and the power of the most stupid. And it is a universal blessing when a species of employment of this kind is within the reach of all, for no one can calculate the amount of good which results when otherwise idle women find occupation for fingers and thought in employments that if not always profitable, are at least innocent and inexpensive.

Still there is much to be done before we can consider the art of knitting to have reached a state of perfection. Books of new designs have appeared by dozens, and many contain exquisitely beautiful patterns, but none of them have done much towards inducing the worker to attain perfection in the art which they profess to teach. Notwithstanding the instructions given, knitters, with very few exceptions, may be said to "amuse themselves sadly." Watch their serious faces, wrinkled foreheads, and round shoulders; listen to the impatient ejaculations which the slightest interruption elicits, and then tell me whether they have just claims to be considered adepts in the art practised with the most complete success by the blind. Assuredly, what woman has done, woman can do; that they do

not do it arises from two causes—they have not considered its possibility, and, con-
sequently, have not tried to do it; and if they did try, they would probably fail,
from their neglecting to cultivate that sense which all alike possess, but which
only the blind seem to use in perfection—the sense of touch.

And touch is of greater service in knitting than all others put together, and which
only requires to be properly disciplined to enable us to leave our eyes, as well as our
thoughts, entirely free, whilst our fingers may be rapidly and accurately engaged in
fabricating any knitted article, however elaborate. This assertion will not appear
exaggerated to those who have had the opportunity of examining the elaborate
handiwork of the inmates of asylums for the blind; nor can it be claimed that the
perfection in their sense of touch is any peculiar gift, since those who have lost
their sight by an accident, as well as those unfortunates who are born blind,
acquire the greatest nicety and dexterity in all kinds of mechanical employments
governed by touch.

It only needs, then, that we should avail ourselves of the marvellous gift of
touch, in order to knit while enjoying the pleasures of conversation, reading the
last new novel, or even studying a foreign tongue.

But to do this, we must begin by selecting proper materials, learning to hold our
work so as to avail ourselves of our power of touch, and carefully cultivating that
sense until we can knit in Egyptian darkness. The slight labor this may at first
demand, will be amply compensated by the increased facility with which we can
pursue our occupation, whilst our duty in social life is no longer neglected for the
sake of poring over our work. In short, we shall soon discover that the exercise
of our sense of touch no more interferes with sight, speech or hearing, than the
sense of smell does, and that it is perfectly and universally practicable to enjoy a
lovely prospect, take part in a lively conversation, or even read aloud, whilst
knitting most busily.

The two principal points to be regarded in knitting are:

First—A judicious selection of materials and implements.

Second—A convenient and elegant method of holding the work.

The directions given for the selection of needles and other materials in all
knitting-books are arbitrary, and demand modifications to suit the fingers of each
individual. Some ladies knit very tightly—others err in the opposite direction—
so that if the two classes were to use the same needles and cotton in knitting a
tidy, one would produce a square hardly large enough to cover a pincushion,
while the work of the other could be used for a bed-spread. To obviate this difficulty, it is always desirable to try a pattern or two with exactly the materials the
knitting-book directs, and judge by the result whether needles are required a size
or two coarser or finer, to give the work the appearance desired.

For edgings, collars, and all narrow work, short needles are more convenient
and elegant than long ones. A knitting-needle housewife, made on the plan of
those for common needles, the flannel divided and numbered for different sizes,
from ten to twenty-four, to roll up and fasten with a button, will be found a most
useful addition to the knitting-box. The knitting gauge and a small piece of
very fine sand-paper for polishing the needles, if rusty, should always be in
readiness.

To Hold the Needle.

The work must be held in the left hand, the needle pressed against the side of
the hand by the third and fourth fingers. The stitches are to be kept near to the
point of the needle by the pressure of the thumb and second finger, and the first

is to be left free to assist in slipping the stitches off, to take, in fact, an active share in the business. A very short practice will enable this finger to ascertain, mechanically, the difference between a purled, a plain, and any other variety of stitch. Indeed, it is principally on the use or neglect of the sense of touch in the forefinger of the left hand that the capacity of knitting, without using the eyes, depends.

The other needle is held between the thumb and first finger of the right hand, and rests on the hand, not under it. The thread is passed loosely round the little finger, under the second and third fingers, and over the tip of the forefinger. The needle is to be held as near the point as possible, the thumb kept as close to the needle as if glued to it, for nothing can be more ungraceful, and at the same time more detrimental to rapid working, than incessant motion of the thumb. The arms and elbows should be perfectly easy, presenting no appearance of stiffness or angularity; and when these rules are observed, no feminine employment is better calculated to display a pretty hand and graceful motion than knitting.

Terms Used in Knitting,

and their explanations, are next to be considered:

To Cast On.—Make a loop in your thread, and place it on the needle in your left hand; when, with your right-hand needle, knit this stitch; but, instead of letting off the first, place the second stitch on the same needle with the first. Repeat this until the desired number of stitches have been made.

To Cast Off.—When a piece of knitting is completed, knit two stitches with the left-hand needle, and pull the first over the second; knit another stitch, pull the first over the second; repeat this till only one stitch remains; draw the thread through this and fasten off securely.

To Increase.—There are a variety of ways of doing this. If one stitch only is to be increased, bring the thread between the needles and knit the following stitch; this will make an open stitch or hole in the following row. If a close increase is to be made, pick up the loop below the next stitch to be knitted, and knit it. To increase one stitch when the row is being seamed, the thread will be in front of the needle; pass it quite round the needle to the front again.

To Decrease.—If one stitch only is to be decreased, knit two stitches together as one; if two stitches are to be decreased, slip one, knit two together, and pass the slipped stitch over the two knit together.

To Fasten On.—Twist the two ends of thread together, and knit a few stitches with both; or a strong weaver's knot answers the purpose.

To Pick Up a Stitch.—With the left-hand needle pick up the loop below the next stitch to be knitted, knit it, and pass it to the other needle.

A Row, is to knit from one end of the needle to the other, once.

Around, is when the stitches are on three needles, to be knit with a fourth; the stitches knit off all three make a round.

To Slip a Stitch, is merely to pass a stitch from the left-hand needle to the right-hand needle without knitting it.

To Seam a Stitch.—Insert the needle in the stitch to be seamed, with the point toward you. Pass the thread quite round the needle; take the needle with the thread on it out at the back; repeat this.

To Knit a Plain Stitch.—Insert the right-hand needle in the stitch to be knitted, with the point from you; pass the thread over the needle, and draw it through to the front; repeat.

To Knit in Ribs, is to knit alternately plain and seamed stitches, either two and three or three and three, according to the width the rib is required.

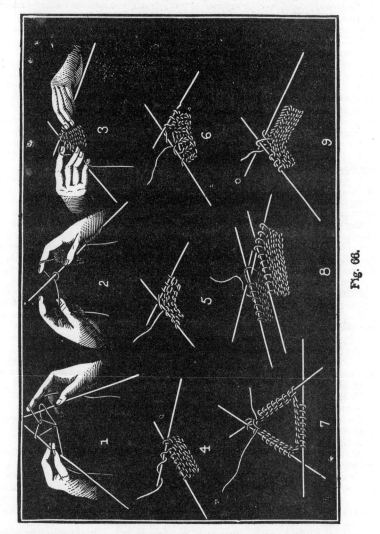

Fig. 66.

To Purl.—The right-hand needle is slipped in the loop in front of the left one, and the thread, after passing between the two, is brought round it; it is then worked as before. The thread is always brought forward before beginning a purled stitch, unless particular directions are given to the contrary.

To Join a Round.—When three needles are used to make a round in knitting, cast one-third of the stitches on the first needle, and slip the second needle in the last stitch, cast on the second third, and do the same with the third needle.

To Join Two Edges.—Divide all the stitches on two needles, hold both in the left hand, and knit with the right-hand needle from each alternately.

To Knit Three Stitches, to Make a Rib of the Centre One.—Slip two off the needle ogether, knit the third, and draw the two others over it.

The accompanying plate will best explain the most important of the stitches just described:

Fig. 1 shows the method of casting on with two needles, which is preferable to using one only, in many kinds of knitting. It has two advantages: it forms a looser stitch, and the stitch is also narrower.

Fig. 2 shows the ordinary method of casting-on with one needle.

Fig. 3 gives the position of the hands in plain knitting, as they appear to the person sitting opposite to the knitter.

Fig. 4 shows the method of making two or more stitches. To make one, merely twist the thread once round the needle; to make more than one, once round for each stitch.

Fig. 5 shows the method of slipping a stitch that is not to be knit.

Fig. 6 shows the method in which the right-hand needle is inserted in the loop for a purled stitch; the thread being previously drawn forward. The thread is then put between the needles towards the front, and so drawn through, as in plain knitting; should the next stitch be in plain knitting, pass the thread to the back again, before knitting it.

Fig. 7 shows the position of three needles on which the stitches are cast when using four; knit two stitches from the third needle to the first to join the round before using the fourth one.

Fig. 8 shows the method of joining two pieces of knitting at the edge, holding both needles in one hand and knitting of each at once to the third.

Fig. 9 shows the method of casting off.

When very long and elaborate pieces of knitting are described, these abbreviations are generally used, but in short descriptions are not required, as they sometimes puzzle inexperienced knitters:

M.—make stitches. P.—purl. K.—knit. K2 tog.—knit two together.

To Knit Two Stitches Together.—This is done in two ways:

First—Put the right-hand needle two loops and knit them as one.

Second—Slip one, knit one, pass slip stitch over the other. In diminishing a diamond, use the second mode for one side, and the first for the other, to give a uniform appearance.

To Knit Three or More Together.—Always slip one, knit two (or more) and pass the slip stitch over.

To Purl Two Together.—Knit two as one.

To Purl Three or More Together.—Slip the first, and pass it over, as in knitting.

Plain Knitting

can be used for an infinite variety of pretty work, suitable for children's occupation, for aged people, and for twilight amusement.

From coarse dishcloths, to be knit in cotton, for kitchen use, to prettier, softer ones, for the toilet; to scarfs, and other straight pieces, little fingers will pass deftly and rapidly to the fancy stitches and more elaborate work.

Fashion's caprices, while constantly suggesting new stitches, leave the old ones always in use. Stockings are knit to-day as our grandmothers knit them, scarfs as our grandfathers wore them in boyhood, while the baby's carriage-blankets and the various head-dresses for evening wrap, are constantly introducing new patterns.

The fashion of covering babies' wee little feet with dainty blankets of finest knitting, while they are taking an airing, has given patterns for many beautiful pieces of work, one of which will be introduced into this chapter.

A Gentleman's Sock.

Three ounces of lamb's-wool yarn are required. The best sized needle is No. 16—steel.

The same pattern, upon very fine needles, in split Berlin wool, makes a very pretty short stocking for a little child just learning to walk.

All stocking knitters require stretchers, which can be obtained at any large housekeeping store. These are wooden shapes of the foot, and come in all sizes. Stockings or socks, when finished, must be dampened and stretched upon them, and not removed until thoroughly dry and in perfect shape.

Cast 28 stitches on the first needle, and 24 on each of the other two.

1st round.—Seam 2, knit 2, repeat; knit 30 rounds in this manner.

31st round.—Seam 1, knit the remainder plain, knit 85 more rounds the same as the last; then for the heel take 18 stitches on each side of the seam, and knit them in rows backwards and forwards, alternately plain and seamed—plain when the right side is towards you, and seamed when the wrong side. Knit 30 rows in this manner, then take 4 on each side the seam-stitch, and place the stitches on each side of these onto separate pins, the centre stitch to be knit and seamed alternately; and at the end of each row knit 2 stitches together from the sides, till there are 17 stitches on the centre pin; then continue knitting those on the centre pin, and with the last stitch of each row take one stitch from the sides, and knit it together with the last as one; when all are knitted off, take up 13 stitches down each side of the heel, knit a plain round, next round decrease by knitting 2 stitches together on each side of the foot; repeat from * five times more, * knit 2 plain rounds in the next, decrease 1 stitch on each side of the foot, repeat from last * three times more, knit 64 plain rounds, divide the stitches for the toe. decrease on each side of 4 stitches on each side of the foot in every alternate round until only 20 stitches remain; place them on two needles, half on each, fold them together, and cast off.

Knit Opera Hood.

Two contrasting colors in Berlin wool, single, are required. For a blonde, white and blue; for a brunette, white and pink, or white and scarlet, would made pretty combinations. The needles should be of ivory, medium sized. Cast on eighty-two stitches with the colored wool, knit one and seam one, repeating until ten rows are knit. Join the white wool, and knit and seam in the same way, after knitting one row plain to conceal the joining. In this way knit alternate stripes, of ten rows each, of colored and white wool, until there are five rows of each knitted.

Now carefully take the first stitch on your needle, drop the second, take the third, drop the fourth, and keep on alternating the stitches taken up and dropped, to the end of the row; keep the first and last stitches on the needle. Knit the half you have kept, very loosely across, and then cast off. Then let the dropped stitches run down, and fasten them neatly. Gather the edge neatly with the ravelled stitches, and finish with a bow of ribbon behind. About one-third is sufficient fullness to fit easily upon the head.

It may be lined with silk, and have broad ribbon strings.

Baby's Shoe.

One ounce each of fine split Berlin wool, pink and white; very fine steel needles. The whole shoe can be knit in white, if preferred, but the foot in colored wool is very pretty, and if done in single wool on one size larger needles, has the effect of a little slipper over a white sock, as shown in the illustration:

Cast on thirty stitches with pink; knit twelve rows, increasing one stitch at the beginning of every row; knit twelve rows, increasing at one end only, for the toe; take thirty stitches on another needle or a piece of thread, and with the remaining eighteen stitches knit thirty-six rows for the toe. Cast on thirty stitches to correspond with the thirty let off; knit twelve rows, decreasing a stitch by knitting two together at the beginning of every alternate row at the toe end; knit twelve more rows, decreasing a stitch at the beginning of every row; thirty stitches will then remain. Take up eighteen stitches with white across the instep on the right side, one between every rib or two

Fig 67.

rows, and an extra one at the beginning and end, quite at the corners, to prevent a little hole that sometimes shows there. The thirty stitches on each side must be taken up on separate needles. The taking up of the stitches across the instep will count as the first row.

2d row.—Knit one, seam eighteen, take a stitch from the side needle, and knit it together with the last as one.

3d row.—Knit one, make one, knit one, make one, knit two together, knit one, knit two together; repeat from first stitch; at the end, knit the last stitch with one off the side needle together as one.

4th row.—Same as second.

5th row.—Knit one, make one, knit three, make one, slip one, knit two together, pass the slipped stitch over; repeat from first stitch; knit the last stitch with one off the side needle.

6th row.—Same as second.

7th row.—Knit one, knit two together, knit one, knit two together, make one, knit one, make one; repeat from first stitch; knit the last stitch, with one off the side needle, together as one stitch.

8th row.—Same as second.

9th row.—Knit one, slip one, knit two together; pass the slipped stitch over, make one, knit three, make one; repeat from first stitch; at the end, knit the last stitch with one off the side needle.

10th row.—Same as second; repeat from the third row twice. This will have taken thirteen stitches from each of the side needles, leaving seventeen on each, and twenty in the centre. Place them all on one needle, and, with the right side of the knitting towards you, knit the whole number of stitches, a plain row.

2d row.—Plain knitting.

3d row.—Cast on a stitch at each end, make one, knit two together; repeat. This is for a row of holes, to run a narrow ribbon in.

Knit the same pattern for the leg as for the instep, beginning at the third row, one stitch to be knitted plain at the beginning and end of every row; repeat the pattern three times, or more if that does not make the leg long enough; knit four plain rows, and cast off; take up the stitches all round the shoe part on three needles, knit two plain rows, and cast off; this is to make it neat where the colors join. Return to the leg, and work into the row of casting off, with the wrong side toward you, a stitch of double crochet, make three chain, miss two loops; repeat.

2d row.—Work a stitch of double crochet into the three chain, make four chain; repeat.

3d row.—Same as second, but five chain, instead of four.

Sew the shoe up neatly, and run a ribbon through the holes. The knitting must be put on a shape to stretch.

An expert knitter can vary the above pattern in many ways, making the shoe into a boot by continuing the colored wool over the instep, and sewing on very tiny buttons, or knitting a band of colored wool, to fasten at the back and be carried across to button round the ankle.

Knitted Counterpane.

The next pattern will be a favorite with those housekeepers who delight in handsome bed-furnishing, as it is beautiful in design, and will outwear a dozen counterpanes bought in stores.

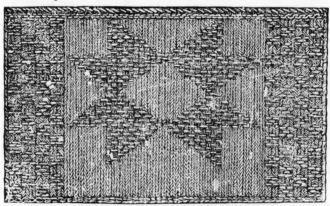

Fig. 63.—KNITTED COUNTERPANE IN STRIPES, WITH BORDER AND FRINGE.

Six pounds of No. 8 three-thread knitting-cotton, and ivory pins, No. 11, are required.

For the stripes that form the centre, cast on 47 stitches.

1st row.—Knit 1, knit 2, seam 2, knit 2, seam 2, knit 7, seam 1, knit 13, seam 1, knit 7, seam 2, knit 2, seam 2, knit 2, knit 1.

2d row.—Knit 1, seam 2, knit 2, seam 2, knit 2, seam 8, knit 1, seam 11, knit 1, seam 8, knit 2, seam 2, knit 2, seam 2, knit 1.

3d row.—Knit 1, seam 2, knit 2, seam 2, knit 2, knit 7, seam 1, knit 1, seam 1, knit 9, seam 1, knit 1, seam 1, knit 7, knit 2, seam 2, knit 2, seam 2, knit 1.

4th row.—Knit 1, knit 2, seam 2, knit 2, seam 2, seam 8, knit 1, seam 1, knit 1, seam 7, knit 1, seam 1, knit 1, seam 8, seam 2, knit 2, seam 2, knit 2, knit 1.

The 9 stitches at the beginning and end of each row that form the border of the stripe must be repeated from the first row, and will not be mentioned again, only the star that forms the centre of the stripe.

5t's row.—After the border stitches, knit 7, seam 1, knit 1, seam 1, knit 1, seam 1, knit 5, seam 1, knit 1, seam 1, knit 1, seam 1, knit 7.

6t's row.—Seam 8, knit 1, seam 1, knit 1, seam 1, knit 1, seam 3, knit 1, seam 1, knit 1, seam 1, knit 1, seam 8.

7t's row.—Knit 7, seam 1, knit 1, seam 1, knit 1, seam 1, knit 1, seam 1, knit 1, seam 1, knit 1, seam 1, knit 1, seam 1, knit 7.

8th row.—Seam 8, knit 1, and seam 1 alternately till 14 are done, seam 7.

9th row.—Knit 1, seam 1, repeat.

10th row.—Seam 2, knit 1, and seam 1 alternately till 11 are done, seam 3, knit 1, and 1 seam 1 alternately till 11 are done, seam 2.

11th row.—Knit 3, seam 1, and knit 1 alternately till 9 are done, knit 5, seam 1, and knit 1 alternately till 9 are done, knit 3.

12th row.—Seam 4, knit 1, and seam 1 alternately till 7 are done, seam 7, knit 1, and seam 1 alternately till 7 are done, seam 4.

13th row.—Knit 5, seam 1, and knit one alternately till 5 are done, knit 9, seam 1, and knit 1 alternately till 5 are done, knit 5.

14th row.—Seam 6, knit 1, seam 1, knit 1, seam 11, knit 1, seam 1, knit 1, seam 6.

15th row.—Knit 7, seam 1, knit 13, seam 1, knit 7.

16th row.—Seam all the stitches.

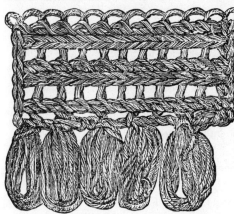

Fig. 69.—FRINGE FOR COUNTERPANE.

3d row.—Knit 6, seam 3; repeat.
4th row.—Knit 4, seam 5; repeat.
5th row.—Knit 4, seam 5; repeat.

6

This forms half the pattern; reverse for the other half, taking the 15th row next, and then the 14th, and so on, till the star is completed. Knit a plain row and a seamed row alternately till 8 are done, still continuing the border on each side; then repeat from the beginning until the stripe is the required length. The stripes can either be sewed or crocheted together.

For the border, cast on 40 stitches, knit 2 plain stitches at the beginning and end of every row. These will not be mentioned again.

1st row.—Knit 8, seam 1; repeat.

2d row.—Knit 2, seam 7; repeat.

6th row.—Knit 6, seam 3; repeat.

7th row.—Knit 2, seam 7; repeat.

8th row.—Knit 8, seam 1; repeat.

Repeat from first row until the border is the length required; it can either be united at the corners or joined straight.

For the fringe, cast on 9 stitches.

1st row.—Make 1, knit 2 together, knit 1; repeat. Make 1, knit 2 together; insert the point of the needle in the last stitch, as if to knit it; wind the cotton over the needle and first and second fingers of the left hand 5 times, the 6th time over the needle only; draw all these loops through the last stitch.

2d row.—Knit all these loops together as one stitch, put the stitch back on the left-hand needle, and seam it very tightly; make 1, seam 2 together, seam 1 make 1, seam 2 together, repeat from third stitch, once.

3d row.—Make 1, knit 2 together, knit 1; repeat twice.

4th row.—Seam 1, make 1, seam 2 together; repeat twice. Repeat from first row, until enough is done to go round the counterpane.

The pattern for the centre can be knit in squares, if preferred to stripes; in that case, 8 rows the same as the side border must be knitted first, and 8 rows, alternately plain and seamed, with the exception of the border, before beginning the star.

Knitted Cloud or Cache-Nez.

Four ounces of Shetland wool and ivory pins, No. 5.

Cast on 334 stitches.

1st row.—Plain knitting.

2d row.—Knit 2, * insert the right-hand needle between the 3d and 4th from the point of left-hand needle, draw the wool through and pass the stitch on to the left-hand needle, repeat from * twice more, knit 2 together 3 times; repeat from first, * at the end knit 2.

3d, 4th, and 5th rows.—Plain knitting.

Repeat from 2d row till the knitting is half a yard wide, cast off, then work the following border in crochet down both sides, but not at the ends.

1st row.—Work 3 long stitches into 1 loop of the casting off, make 1 chain, miss 3 loops; repeat.

2d row.—Work 1 long stitch into the 1 chain-stitch in the last row, make 3 chain and repeat.

3d row.—Work 3 long stitches into the centre one of the 3 chain in last row, make 1 chain, miss 3 loops, and repeat.

4th row.—Work one long stitch into every loop.

5th row.—Work 7 stitches of double crochet into successive loops, make 9 chain, miss 6 loops, and repeat.

6th row.—Work 5 stitches of double crochet into successive loops, beginning on the 2d of the 7 in last row, make 9 chain in last row, make 7 chain, and repeat.

7th row.—Work 3 stitches of double crochet into successive loops, beginning on the 2d of the 5 in last row, make 7 chain, work 3 long stitches into successive loops, beginning on the chain before the 1 long stitch in last row, make 7 chain, and repeat.

8th row.—Work 1 stitch of double crochet over the centre one of the 3 in last row, make 5 chain, work 1 long stitch into the 7 chain-stitches in last row, make 5 chain, work 1 long stitch into the centre one of the 3 long stitches in last row, make 5 chain, work 1 long stitch into the 7 chain-stitches, make 5 chain, and repeat.

9th row.—Work 1 long stitch into the 5 chain-stitches, before the stitch of

Fig. 70.—BLANKET FOR INFANT'S CARRIAGE.

double crochet in last row, work 1 long stitch into the 5 chain-stitches after the stitch of double crochet, make 4 chain, work 1 long stitch into the next 5 chain, make 5 chain, work 1 long stitch into the next 5 chain, make 4 chain, and repeat; work the same down the other side, then draw up the ends, and add a long, heavy tassel, made of the wool, at each end. These clouds are very popular both for evening and sea-side wear, and are universally becoming.

Blanket for Infant's Carriage.

The abbreviations will be found explained in this chapter, and the pattern will be found very beautiful. This style of work is usually termed knitted embroidery, and is popular for breakfast shawls, sacques and much ornamental work. Books containing patterns are sold at all fancy stores.

The plate (Fig. 70) gives a section of the blanket, sufficiently large to distinguish its component parts.

It consists of a centre, surrounded by an open border; then a border of forget-me-nots, with rose-bud sprays as corner pieces, a narrow and a wider open border, and a Vandyke edge.

The first part to be done is the border of forget-me-nots, to secure the whole of the pattern being perfect.

Begin where the flower leans towards the right; thus each of the four sides is considered to begin at the left-hand corner.

The materials are No. 14 ivory needles, and double Berlin wool, blue, yellow, green and white.

Cast on 60 stitches.

Plain knitting with every alternate row purled.

The same may be said of all knotted embroidery, the self-colored parts only, such as centres of scarfs, being knit in patterns.

1st row, 3 white, 1 green, 56 white.
2d, 51 w, 1 g, 3 w, 1 g, 4 w.
3d, 5 w, 1 g, 1 w, 4 g, 49 w.
4th, 48 w, 6 g, 6 w.
5th. 7 w, 6 g, 47 w.
6th, 46 w, 7 g, 7 w.
7th, 7 w, 7 g, 46 w.
8th, 25 w, 2 g, 13 w, 7 g, 8 w.
9th, 8 w, 7 g, 9 w, 10 g, 26 w.
10th, 27 w, 11 g, 6 w, 7 g, 9 w.
11th, 9 w, 8 g, 4 w, 11 g, 28 w.
12th, 29 w, 11 g, 1 w, 2 g, 1 w, 6 g, 10 w.
13th, (begin blue), 11 w, 5 g, 3 w, 11 g, 4 w, 1 blue, 25 w.
14th, 24 w, 3 b, 5 w, 7 g, 5 w, 4 g, 12 w.
15th, 13 w, 2 g, 7 w, 5 g, 5 w, 5 b, 23 w.
16th, 22 w, 1 b, 1 w, 3 b, 1 w, 1 b, 15 w, 2 g, 14 w.
17th, 16 w, 1 g, 13 w, 3 b, 1 w, 1 b, 1 w, 3 b, 21 w.
18th, (begin yellow), 20 w, 5 b, 1 yellow, 5 b, 10 w, 2 g, 17 w.
19th, 16 w, 1 g, 2 w, 1 g, 10 w, 3 b, 1 w, 1 b, 1 w, 3 b, 21 w.
20th, 22 w, 1 b, 1 w, 3 b, 1 w, 1 b, 6 w, 1 g, 1 w, 2 g, 2 w, 3 g, 16 w.
21st, 14 w, 5 g, 3 w, 1 g, 9 w, 5 b, 23 w.
22d, 24 w, 3 b, 8 w, 2 g, 3 w, 7 g, 13 w.
23d, 13 w, 7 g, 3 w, 1 g, 1 w, 2 g, 7 w, 1 b, 25 w.
24th, 21 w, 1 b, 9 w, 2 g, 2 w, 1 g, 3 w, 8 g, 13 w.
25th, 13 w, 8 g, 4 w, 1g, 3 w, 2 g, 6 w, 3 b, 13 w, 3 g, 4 w.
26th, 5 w, 6 g, 8 w, 5 b, 3 w, 2 g, 4 w, 1 g, 5 w, 7 g, 14 w.

27th, 13 w, 7 g, 6 w, 1 g, 6 w, 2 g, 1 b, 1 w, 3 b, 1 w, 1 b, 5 w, 6 g, 7 w.
28th, 9 w, 6 g, 2 w, 3 b, 1 w, 1 b, 1 w, 3 b, 6 w, 2 g, 7 w, 5 g, 14 w.
29th, 15 w, 3 g, 9 w, 1 g, 1 b, 4 w, 5 b, 1 yellow, 5 b, 6 g, 10 w.
30th, 17 w, 3 b, 1 w, 1 b, 1 w, 3 b, 4 w, 3 b, 9 w, 4 g, 14 w.
31st, 15 w, 2 g, 9 w, 5 b, 4 w, 1 b, 1 w, 3 b, 5 w, 1 b, 5 w, 1 b, 4 w, 1 b, 7 w.
32d, 8 w, 3 g, 3 b, 4 w, 1 g, 5 b, 4 w, 1 b, 1 w, 3 b, 1 w, 1 b, 8 w, 3 g, 14 w.
33d, 15 w, 1 g, 8 w, 3 b, 1 w, 1 b, 1 w, 3 b, 4 w, 3 b, 2 w, 1 g, 2 w, 5 b, 10 w.
34th, 9 w, 1 b, 1 w, 3 b, 1 w, 1 b, 1 g, 4 w, 1 b, 4 w, 5 b, 1 yellow, 5 b, 23 w.
35th, 24 w, 3 b, 1 w, 1 b, 1 w, 3 b, 6 w, 1 g, 3 w, 3 b, 1 w, 1 b, 1 w, 3 b, 8 w.
36th, 7 w, 5 b, 1 yellow, 5 b, 1 w, 2 g, 7 w, 1 b, 1 w, 3 b, 1 w, 1 b, 25 w.
37th, 26 w, 5 b, 8 w, 3 g, 1 w, 3 b, 1 w, 1 b, 1 w, 3 b, 8 w.
38th, 9 w, 1 b, 1 w, 3 b, 1 w, 1 b, 1 w, 4 g, 9 w, 3 b, 27 w.
39th, 28 w, 1 b, 10 w, 4 g, 2 w, 5 b, 10 w.
40th, 10 w, 1 g, 3 b, 3 w, 4 g, 39 w.
41st, 3 w, 1 g, 35 w, 4 g, 7 w, 1 g, 1 w, 1 g, 7 w.
42d, 6 w, 3 g, 9 w, 3 g, 29 w, 2 g, 3 w, 1 g, 4 w.
43d, 5 w, 1 g, 1 w, 4 g, 29 w, 1 g, 10 w, 4 g, 5 w.
44th, 5 w, 4 g, 39 w, 6 g, 6 w.
45th, 7 w, 6 g, 39 w, 4 g, 4 w.
46th, 4 w, 3 g, 39 w, 7 g, 7 w.
47th, 7 w, 7 g, 39 w, 3 g, 4 w.
48th, 4 w, 1 g, 20 w, 2 g, 18 w, 7 g, 8 w.
49th, 8 w, 7 g, 9 w, 10 g, 21 w, 1 g, 4 w.
50th, 27 w, 11 g, 6 w, 7 g, 9 w.

You will find, at the completion of the 50th row, that you have made one complete bunch of " Forget-me-Nots," and done 10 rows of the 2d bunch. After this you will repeat, between the 11th and 50th rows inclusive, for as many bunches as you may require, taking care not to make the commencement of the new group, when working the last 10 rows of the one that terminates that side of the border. The engraver has represented the sprays of flowers leaning in opposite directions, and meeting in the centre of each border. This is unnecessary; but being, perhaps, more uniform, you may as well know how to do it. Having completed the 50th (which is a purled row), knit one row plain, and then knit as follows, the 1st row being purled, and the 2d and other alternate plain:—

1st reverse, 4w, 1 g, 55 w.
2d do., 55 w, 1 g, 4 w.
3d do., 4 w, 3 g, 53 w.
4th do., 53 w, 3 g, 4 w.
5th do., 4 w, 4 g, 52 w.
6th do., 51 w, 4 g, 5 w.
7th do., 40 w, 1 g, 10 w, 4 g, 5 w.
8th do., 6 w, 3 g, 9 w, 3 g, 39 w.
9th do., 39 w, 4 g, 4 w, 1 *blue*, 2 w, 1 g, 1 w, 1 g, 7 w.

The next row is like the 40th, and you will now work the former receipt *backwards*, until you have knitted the 10th; then knit from the 49th to the 10th inclusive, until you come to the last spray in that side of the border, when you will knit from the 9th to the 1st row inclusive, instead of going from the 10th to the 49th.

This pattern would be extremely beautiful for the borders of a lady's scarf, knitted in Pyrenees or Berlin wool, with a black or other dark ground; it would also make a most elegant neck-tie, knitted in fine netting silk, the ground being crimson, amber, or a rich Adelaide brown. In either case it is imperative that the sprays should be knitted reversely from the centre; and the ends of the neck-ribbon should be finished with a rich fringe, to correspond with the colors of the flowers.

Ombre silks and wools may be used with excellent effect, both in the blues and the greens.

Open Hem Borders.

Double Berlin wool of a soft fawn color. Needles as before. Cast on twenty-five stitches.

1st row.—× K 1, m 1, k 2 tog., k 1, k 2 tog., k 1, k 2 tog., m 1. × 4 times, k 1.

2d row.—P 2 tog., × m 1, p 3, m 1, p 3 tog., repeat 4 times, but p 2 tog. last time.

3d row.—× k 2, m 1, k 3 tog., m 1, k 1, × 4 times, k 1.

4th row.—× p 1, p 2 tog., m 1, p 1, m 1, p 2 tog., × 4 times, p 1.

This completes one pattern. Repeat. Of the other two open-hem borders, the outer is done in the same wool as this one, but with thirteen stitches only; the narrow is in deep blue, and you will cast on 7 stitches; both are done in this pattern.

Centre.

Cast on a sufficient number of stitches to make the length of the vacant space in the centre, taking care to be able to divide them by 8 and have 1 over.

1st row, × k 1, p 7 ×, repeat, k 1.

2d, P 2, × k 5, p 3, × repeat, k 5, p 2 at the end.

3d, K 3, × p 3, k 5, × repeat, p 3, k 3 at the end.

4th, P 4, × k 1, p 7 ×, repeat, k 1, p 4 at the end.

5th, as 4th

6th, as 3d.

7th, as 2d.

8th, as 1st.

Repeat these eight rows until sufficient is done to fill up the oblong in the centre; the pattern consists of oblong diamonds, of which the lower half is knitted, and the upper purled. The effect is very pretty. The engraver has represented its appearance exactly.

Rosebud Corners.

The engraving gives so exact a representation of this beautiful group of rose-buds, that it will be by no means difficult to knit from it; allowing it to be a perfect square, 85 rows deep, and casting on 85 stitches; of course the forget-me-not border will be joined to it on each side, without interfering with the square of the rosebuds.

I have allowed two stitches more than the engraving gives, that the extremities of the pattern may not approach the edge too closely, and that number of rows being 25 more than are required for the smaller flowers, will admit of the *open-hem border*, exactly filling up the vacant space.

The colors required for the rosebud corners are green and two shades of rose, with white for the ground. The parts where the lightest shade of pink is to be knitted in are represented in the engraving by faint diagonal lines; the remaining parts of each bud are to be in the darker shade, and the *white* squares everywhere indicate green.

You will perceive that this square is to be knitted four times over, and then placed in different positions, to make the corners correspond, the three buds leaning to the centre.

This pattern, knitted in Berlin or Pyrenees wool, will form a splendid corner for a knitted shawl, the ground being black. The border of the shawl may be knitted in the forget-me-not, or any other pattern you like. In this case, various shades of green should be employed, to give the nearest approach to nature; the centre may be made in the open-hem pattern I have given, or any other which presents a tolerably smooth surface; but such patterns as the *double rose-leaf* and the *leaf and trellis* are very unfit for knitted embroidery in wool, because the chenille-like effect it should produce is lost.

Knitted shawls need be only half-squares, but should be lined with silk and wadded.

These patterns might also be used as the borders of a lady's scarf for the neck, forget-me-nots being knitted *all round*, and the spray of rosebuds at each end of the centre.

Both shawls and scarfs must be finished oft with a deep fringe.

Vandyke Border.

Berlin wool, deep pink and white.
The 1st Vandyke is entirely white, cast on 9 stitches.
The first row, k 3, × m 2, k 2 together, × twice, m 2, k 2.
2d, k 3, p 1, k 2, p 1, k 2, p 1, k 3.
3d, plain knitting.
4th, k 2, m 2, k 3 tog., m 4, k 3 tog., k 2, m 2, k 2 tog., k 1.
5th, k 3, p 1, k 4, p 1, k 1, p 1, k 2, p 1, k 2.
6th, Plain knitting.
7th, K 3, m 2, k 4 tog., × m 2, k 2 tog., × 4 times, k 1.
8th, K 3, p 1, × k 2, p 1, × 4 times, k 3.
9th, Plain knitting.
10th, Cast off 8; knit the remainder.
The next row begins the pink Vandyke.

Pink Vandyke.

1st row, 9 white, 2 p.
2d, Knit 2 pink, purl 9 white.
3d, Knit 8 white, 1 pink on white, (pink) m 1, k 2.
4th, (P) k 2, p 2, (w) p 8.
5th, (W) k 7, (p) k 1 w and 1 p together, m 1, k 1, m 1, k 2.
6th, (P) k 2, p 4, (w) p 7.
7th, (W) k 6, (p) k 1, w and 1 p together, m 1, k 3, m 1, k 2.
8th, (P) k 2, p 6, (w) p 6.
9th, (W) k 5, (p) k 2 together as before, m 1, k 2, m 1, k 2 tog., k 1, m 1, k 2.
10th, (P) knit 2, p 8, (w) p 5.
11th, (W) k 4, (p) k 2 together, m 1, k 1, k 2 tog., m 1, k 1, m 1, k 2 tog., k 1, m 1, k 2.
12th, (P) k 2, p 10, (w) p 4.
13th, (W) k 3, (p) 2 together, m 1, k 1, k 2 tog., m 1. k 3, m 1, k 2 tog., k 1, 1, k 2.
14th, (P) k 2, p 12, (w) p 3.

15*th*, (W) k 2, (p) k 2 together, m 1, k 1, k 2 tog., m 1, k 2, × m 1, k 2 tog., k 1, × twice, m 1, k 2.

16*th*, (P) k 2, p 14, (w) p 2.

17*th*, (W) k 1, (p) k 2 tog., k 1, m 1, k 2 tog., k 1, m 1, k 2 tog., k 2 tog., k 1, × m 1, k 2 tog., k 1, × repeat.

18*th*, (P) k 2, p 12, (w) p 2.

19*th*, (W) k 3, (p) k 1, m 1, k 2 tog., k 1, m 1, k 3 tog., × m 1, k 2 tog., k 1, × twice.

20*th*, (P) k 2, p 10, (w) p 3.

21*st*, (W) k 4, (p) k 1, m 1, k 2 tog., k 2 tog., × m 1, k 2 tog., k 1, × twice.

22*d*, (P) k 2, p 8, (w) p 4.

23*d*, (W) k 5, (p) k 1, m 1, k 2 tog., k 1, k 2 tog., m 1, k 2 tog., k 1.

24*th*, (P) k 2, p 6, (w) p 5.

25*th*, (W) k 6, (p) k 1, m 1, k 3 tog., m 1, k 2 tog., k 1.

26*th*, (P) k 2, p 4, (w) p 6.

27*th*, (W) k 7, (p) k 2 tog., m 1, k 2 tog., k 1.

28*th*, (P) k 2, p 2, (w) p 7.

29*th*, All white. K 7, k 2 tog., twice.

30*th*, Purled.

Cut off the pink wool, leaving about three inches, and repeat the white Vandyke, then the pink, and so on, until sufficient is done to go round the blanket, slightly full. Terminate with pink Vandyke.

Border for a Knit Sacque or Breakfast Shawl.

Three colors are required for the pattern of this border, besides the groundwork, which should be that of the body of the sacque. They are a rich bright green, olive green, and brilliant scarlet; or, by way of variety, the scarlet may be exchanged for blue.

Fig. 71.

As it is desirable that the running border should be much wider in the skirt than in the body, it is necessary to procure Shetland wools of exactly the same shades as the Berlin; and by knitting the pieces to trim the body with Shetland wool and finer needles, and for the skirts with Berlin and coarse needles, you will produce the same trimmings of different widths.

The pattern is as follows:

(S), *scarlet ;* (o g), *olive green ;* (g), *green ;* (b), *brown,* for the ground, (or *black* if it is preferred).

Cast on 40 stitches, with two needles.

1st row, 3 b, 12 g, 2 b, 5 g, 2 b, 2 o g, 1 b, 1 o g, 1 b, 4 s, 7 b.

2d, 6 b, 6 s, 3 o g, 2 b, 1 o g, 20 g, 2 b.

3d, 1 b, 21 g, 1 o g, 2 b, 2 o g, 1 b, 6 s, 6 b.

4th, 7 b, 4 s, 3 b, 1 o g, 1 b, 2 o g, 20 g, 2 b.

5th, 3 b, 12 g, 2 b, 5 g, 2 o g, 1 b, 1 o g, 4 b, 2 s, (break off the scarlet), 8 b.

6th, 14 b, 3 o g, 1 b, 5 g, 3 b, 10 g, 4 b.

7th, 6 b, 7 g, 3 b, 6 g, 2 b, 2 o g, 14 b.

8th, 14 b, 1 o g, 4 b, 6 g, 3 b, 4 g. 8 b.

9th, 10 b, 1 g, 3 b, 7 g, 4 b, 1 o g, 14 b.

10th, 14 b, 2 o g, 4 b, 8 g, 12 b.

11th, 11 b, 9 g, 4 b, 1 o g, 15 b.

12th, 15 b, 1 o g, 5 b, 9 g 10 b.

13th, 9 b, 9 g, 6 b, 1 o g, 15 b.

14th, 15 b, 2 o g, 6 b, 7 g, 10 b.

15th, 11 b, 6 g, 6 b, 1 o g, 16 b.

16th, 16 b, 2 o g, 7 b, 3 g, 12 b.

17th, 13 b, 2 g, 6 b, 3 o g, 16 b.

18th, 13 b, 1 g, 3 b, 2 o g, 7 b, 1 g, 13 b.

19th, 20 b, 2 o g, 3 b, 2 g, 13 b.

20th, 12 b, 3 g. 4 b, 2 o g, 10 b, 2 s, 7 b.

21st, 6 b, 4 s, 7 b, 3 o g, 3 b, 6 g, 11 b.

22d, 11 b, 6 g, 3 b, 3 o g, 6 b, 6 s, 5 b.

23d, 5 b, 6 s, 6 b, 2 o g, 3 b, 8 g, 10 b.

24th, 10 b, 9 g, 3 b, 2 o g, 6 b, 4 s, 6 b.

25th, 7 b, 2 s, 7 b, 1 o g, 3 b, 9 g, 11 b.

26th, 12 b, 8 g, 3 b, 1 o g, 6 b, 1 o g, 4 b, 2 s, 3 b.

27th, 2 b, 4 s, 3 b, 1 o g, 5 b, 2 o g, 2 b. 7 g, 3 b, 1 g, 10 b.

28th, 8 b, 4 g, 3 b, 6 g, 3 b, 1 o g, 4 b, 1 o g, 2 b, 1 o g, 6 s, 1 b.

29th, 1 b, 6 s, 1 b, 2 o g, 1 b, 1 o g, 3 b, 1 o g, 3 b, 5 g, 3 b, 7 g, 6 b.

30th, 4 b, 10 g, 3 b, 5 g, 2 b, 1 o g, 2 b, 2 o g, 1 b, 1 o g, 3 b, 4 s, 2 b.

31st, 3 b, 2 s, 2 b, 2 s, 3 b, 1 o g, 1 b, 2 o g, 2 b, 5 g, 2 b, 12 g, 3 b.

32d, 2 b, 21 g, 2 b, 3 o g, 2 b, 4 s, 6 b.

33d, 5 b, 6 s, 2 b, 2 o g, 2 b, 22 g, 1 b.

34th, 2 b, 21 g, 2 b, 1 o g, 3 b, 6 s, 5 b.

35th, 6 b, 4 s, 4 b, 1 o g, 1 b, 1 o g, 6 g, 2 b, 12 g, 3 b.

36th, 4 b, 10 g, 3 b, 5 g, 1 b, 3 o g, 5 b, 2 s, 7 b.

37th, 14 b, 2 o g, 2 b, 6 g, 3 b, 7 g, 6 b.

38th, 8 b, 4 g, 3 b, 6 g, 4 b, 1 g, 14 b.

39th, 14 b, 1 o g, 4 b, 7 g, 3 b, 1 g, 10 b.

40th, 12 b, 8 g, 4 b, 2 o g, 14 b.

41st, 15 b, 1 o g, 4 b, 8 g, 12 b.

42d, 11 b, 8 g, 5 b, 1 o g, 15 b.

43d, 15 b, 1 o g, 6 b, 8 g, 10 b.

44th, 10 b, 7 g, 6 b, 2 o g, 15 b.

45th, 16 b, 1 o g, 6 b, 6 g, 11 b.

46th, 12 b, 3 g, 7 b, 2 o g, 4 b, 1 g, 11 b.

47th, 11 b, 2 g, 3 b, 3 o g, 6 b, 2 g, 13 b.

48th, 13 b, 1 g, 7 b, 2 o g, 4 b, 3 g, 10 b.

49th, 9 b, 6 g, 3 b, 2 o g, 20 b.
50th, 9 b, 2 *scarlet*, 8 b, 2 o g, 4 b, 7 g, 8 b.
51st, 8 b, 9 g. 2 b, 2 o g. 7 b, 4 s, 8 b.
52d, 7 b, 6 s, 5 b, 2 o g, 3 b, 8 g, 9 b.
53d, 10 b, 8 g, 3 b, 1 o g, 5 b, 6 s, 7 b.
54th, 3 b, 2 s, 3 b, 4 s, 5 b, 2 o g, 2 b, 9 g, 10 b.
55th, 11 b, 9 g, 2 b, 1 o g, 6 b, 2 s, 3 b, 4 s, 2 b.
56th, 1 b, 6 s, 2 b, 1 o g, 6 b, 2 o g, 2 b, 7 g, 13 b.
57th, 10 b, 1 g, 3 b, 7 g, 2 b, 1 o g, 5 b, 1 o g, 1 b, 2 o g, 6 s. 1 b.
58th, 2 b, 4 s, 3 b, 2 o g, 5 b, 1 o g, 2 b, 6 g, 3 b, 4 g, 8 b.
59th, 6 b, 7 g, 3 b, 5 g, 2 b, 2 o g, 3 b, 3 o g, 4 b, 2 s, 3 b.
60th, 7 b, 2 s, 2 b, 2 o g, 2 b, 1 o g. 3 b, 4 g, 3 b, 10 g, 4 b.
The 60th row completes one pattern. It will be necessary to knit the piece which is to be inserted in the skirt before knitting the skirt itself, in order that the patterns may join exactly. When you have knitted the 60th row of the last pattern, cast off with brown wool; break off the ends of the other colors, and fasten them off carefully with an embroidery needle. Take particular care in joining this pattern that the two ends shall correspond exactly.

Fig. 72.—SOFA CUSHION.

The band is to be knitted in Shetland wool.
Shaded green will look well for the leaves and stems, but I prefer the berries of one bright shade.
To make up all articles in knitted embroidery, cut out the exact shape of every part in paper, and then knit the trimmings. Mark on the paper the space they occupy, and knit the remaining parts in a seef color, either in plain knitting or in any fancy stitch you prefer. Knit the waist and sleeves to the paper pattern, increasing or diminishing, as the size requires.
It is impossible to give the number of stitches to be cast on in the different plain parts of this style of knitting. Necessarily this must depend upon the size of the article required, size of needles, and many other things.

Sofa Cushion in Knitted Embroidery.

The groundwork of this cushion, Fig. 72, is of deep crimson, and the pattern in shaded brown Berlin wool. Lined with damask, and trimmed with silk cord and tassels.

Satchel in Knitting and Embroidery.

This satchel is made of dark cloth, embroidered in colors, and made up over leather. The top is of Berlin wool, knit in stripes, and finished with a steel clasp and leather handles.

Fig. 73.

CHAPTER IX.

CROCHET WORK.

Crochet work, a species of knitting originally practised by the peasants in Scotland with a small hooked needle, called a shepherd's hook, has, aided by taste and fashion, obtained a popularity second to no other kind of fancy work. It derives its present name from the French; the needle with which it is worked being by them, from its crooked shape, termed "crochet."

This art has attained its highest degree of perfection in the elaborate and beautiful articles now made, as it is applied to almost every article that can be produced in knitting or embroidery.

Shawls, table-covers, couvrepieds, pillows, ottomans, footstools, mats, slippers, purses, unlimited numbers of pretty articles are constantly made in this work.

Silk, wool, cotton, chenille, and gold thread are all suitable materials for this description of work, but the purpose for which each article is intended must determine the choice of material.

Crochet has the recommendation of being a less intricate method of working than knitting, and one great advantage it possesses is that, if hastily laid aside the stitches do not slip as in knitting. It can be worked in thread as fine as a cobweb for imitation lace, in heaviest double wool for carriage rugs, or in strong twine for horse blankets, and between the lace and horse blanket the range of stitch and work is unlimited.

Shawls, sleeves, comforters, mittens, gloves, etc., may be made, without difficulty, in crochet. It has not, however, been deemed necessary in the following pages to give directions for any of these simple articles, as, when the crochet stitch is acquired, the modes of working such, and a variety of others, in daily use, will readily present themselves. As an example of the double appropriation, which almost all the following directions admit of, we may instance the bottom of a bag; this, if commenced with a chain of about fifty stitches (not joining the ends), and worked in coarse wool, with a large needle, in rows backwards and forwards, gradually increasing with a seam stitch, will form a warm and comfortable round cape. A paper pattern, the size of any desired object, can easily be cut—and the making a stitch at the commencement, or the decreasing in the middle, or the end of a row, and *vice versa*, render this work subservient to almost any form.

For large pieces of work, when wool is employed, that kind denominated fleecy, either English or German, is generally to be preferred. This material, of a six-thread size, with an ivory needle, offers the easiest kind of work with which wo are acquainted. It may be readily learned, and has, therefore, been much practised, both by invalids, and by persons whose sight either needs relief, or has become impaired. All striped patterns, if desired, may be worked in narrow breadths, and joined in the dividing lines; so that a table cover may be made in four or six lengths, and afterwards sewn together with wool, without the least detriment to its appearance. Crochet may be executed with coarse and fine chenille, for pillows, bags, caps, and waistcoats; with crochet silk, for caps, slippers, and bags; with coarse netting silk, it forms strong purses, bags, and slippers; and the most delicate work may be done with the finer silks. Gold and silver cord, and passing, may be intermixed with the chenilles and silks, or employed separately; and gold and steel beads, first strung on the silk, may be worked in various patterns, so as to produce the most rich and beautiful effect.

Crochet may be divided into plain single crochet, plain double crochet, plain stitch open crochet, and open crochet with one, two, three, or more stitches. These varieties will be described, as they occur, in the following directions for working.

The mode of working the crochet stitch, although in itself most simple, is difficult to describe in writing; but, with the aid of the annexed engraving, which shows the position of the hands, and the manner in which the needle and the work should be held, we will endeavor to explain the elementary process.

Having wound a skein of wool, make a loop at one end; through this loop draw another loop, through this second loop another, and so on, moderately tightening each, as it is drawn through, until a chain of sufficient length be made to serve as the foundation for the article intended to be worked. Pass the needle through the last loop of this foundation, and catching the wool, draw it through, repeating the same at every successive loop; then, return along this row, and, in a similar manner, form a second. A repetition of this process, alternately backwards and forwards, from right to left, and from left to right, will give the first and easiest lessons. The work will be the same on both sides, producing by turns one raised and one sunken row.

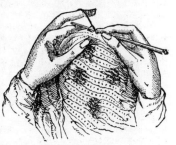

Fig 74.

Before proceeding further, however, it will be found useful to examine the plate and description of the usual stitches.

The stitches used in crochet are. CHAIN-STITCH, SLIP-STITCH, SINGLE CROCHET, (Sc.), DOUBLE CROCHET, TREBLE CROCHET (Tc.), LONG TREBLE, (Long Tc.). We also speak occasionally of working *through* a stitch.

CHAIN-STITCH is the foundation of all other crochet. A loop is made on the hook, and through this the thread is drawn. A second loop being thus made, the thread is drawn through it; and so on, until the required number of chain-stitches is made. Observe that we never reckon the first loop in counting a chain.

SLIP-STITCH.—A chain being made, the hook is inserted in the last stitch but one to that already on the needle, and the thread drawn through both together; then in the next stitch, and so on. In working back a chain in *slip-stitch*, you will always work one stitch less than the number of the chain, because the last of the chain is missed before the first slip is worked. This stitch adds but little to the width of work, and is, therefore, very useful to strengthen the veins of leaves, and to bring the thread to some new point. Slip-stitch is also

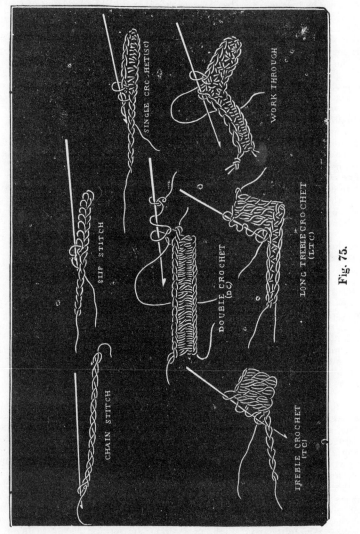

Fig. 75.

used in the Honiton lace, to finish off each leaf and flower before proceeding with the stem. The hook is put through the thickest part, close to the stem, and the thread drawn through it and the loop on the needle together, which renders it firm and neat.

SINGLE CROCHET (Sc.)—In this the thread is drawn through the chain of the last row, and forms a second loop on the needle. Through the two loops the thread is drawn by a *single* movement.

DOUBLE CROCHET (Dc.)—The thread is passed *once* over the needle, before the hook is inserted in the chain through which the thread is drawn ; there will thus be *three* loops on the needle. Draw the thread through *two*, which leaves *one* and *the new loop*. Draw the thread through these; thus, by the double movement, completing the stitch.

TREBLE CROCHET (Tc.) is worked precisely like Dc.; but the thread being put *twice* over the needle, instead cf *once*, the stitch is completed by drawing the thread *three* times through two loops.

LONG TREBLE CROCHET (Long Tc.)—Like Tc., except that the thread is twisted *three* times round the needle, and drawn four successive times through two loops.

When directions are given to work a stitch *through* another, you must put the hook under both threads of the last row. A glance at the engraving will, however, explain this stitch more clearly than any words I can use.

To CLOSE A LOOP, pass the needle through the stitch directed, and draw the thread through that and the loop already on the needle; as this takes up one stitch, one less than the number marked will be the actual size of every loop; thus, a chain of *sixteen* for *Open Leaf* (see first sprig) leaves *fifteen* to be worked round.

In working a flower or leaf, pass the thread under the stem, and keep the needle above it, for each new round.

To FASTEN OFF.—Cut off the thread about three inches from the work. Draw the end through the last stitch, and, with a common needle, run it up and down a few threads, invisibly, at the back. Do the same with the end left when the work was begun, and cut off close.

The size of the crochet work depends entirely upon the style of working. One person does crochet work in a very tight stitch, others very loosely, and a few stitches had better be tried for every article before selecting the hook.

Examine carefully the form of the needle, and try the hook to ascertain that it is perfectly smooth. Some are so sharp and rough as to tear any of the usual threads in use.

Select those which are not of uniform thickness up to the hook. The best are those which are thinner there than an inch farther up. Where the needle is not proportionably fine near the hook, it is almost impossible to keep the work even.

Chain-stitch ought to be done rather loosely, as working on it afterwards contracts it, and is apt to give it a puckered appearance. It is often advisable to use a needle one size larger for making the chain than for the rest of the work, especially in edgings. It will be found much easier to work the succeeding rows when this precaution is taken.

Crochet needles should be kept in a housewife similar to those used for ordinary needles. The slightest soil or rust should be effaced with fine sand-paper.

A steel crochet needle is generally advisable ; with expert workers, it makes the most even stitches, but an ivory needle is easier to work with.

The second sized netting silk is prettiest for purses.

The coarsest, or crochet silk, is best adapted for bags, with steel or gold beads. Where many colors are required in a pattern, and the same do not very frequently occur, it is advisable to introduce them in short lengths, instead of carrying on each thread. This should always be attended to when working with chenille.

When beads are used, they should be strung on the silk with a needle.

When beads are introduced, the wrong side of the work becomes the right. It is possible to crochet with the beads on the right side, but they never lay so firmly, nor indeed is it the proper way of using them.

The average number of stitches for the length of a purse, in fine silk, is one hundred and sixty. In coarse silk, one hundred and ten.

From ninety to one hundred stitches form the circle of a purse in fine silk.

One hundred and thirty stitches may be taken for the round of a bag, in crochet silk.

A table-cover, in six-thread fleecy, is generally computed at about four hundred stitches in length.

Borders of flowers, and very intricate patterns, may be worked in crochet, but it would be impossible to convey a complete idea of these even to the most experienced worker, unless accompanied with colored patterns, which the nature of our illustrations precludes us from offering. The expert needlewoman will soon perceive the best method of copying any pattern of this description she may desire.

The terms chine and ombre, are frequently applied to the materials employed in crochet and knitting. Wool and silk are chine, when two, three, or more different colors are introduced, at intervals, on one thread, in the process of dying; they are ombre, when one color only is similarly employed, but which gradually runs from the lightest to the darkest shade.

N. B. In the directions for working the different patterns in crochet, it must be borne in mind, that unless any other stitch be mentioned, the plain, or double crochet stitch is always to be employed.

A Sofa Pillow, or Table-cover.

This is given as the first and easiest pattern in crochet, for the purpose of teaching the stitch.

A good sized ivory or steel crochet needle, with six-thread fleecy, will be required. Instead of working the rows backwards and forwards, as before described, begin each row separately at the same end. When the last stitch of each row is finished, draw the wool through, and cut it off, leaving an end of two or three inches. It is impossible to determine the exact number of stitches—that must depend on the article, and its required size; but with this description of wool, half a yard in length will generally be found to number about sixty-five stitches, and a calculation may accordingly be made.

1st stripe—one row black ; one row white ; one row black.

2d stripe—one row dark scarlet; one bright scarlet; one light scarlet; reverse the same, to form a shaded stripe.

3d stripe—the same as the first.

4th stripe—the same as the second, but in shades of blue.

These stripes are to be repeated alternately.

Another Very Easy Pattern.

The ground of this pattern is plain. The cheques are composed of chine wool, the first row differing in color from that of the second. The dividing line is in plain colors.

This pattern may be worked in stripes of different colors, varying the color of tho cheques agreeably to that of the ground. It is adapted for a pillow, o. a variety of other articles, according to the material employed.

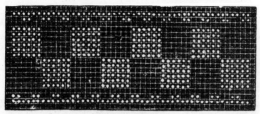

Fig. 76.

Gentlemen's Crochet Silk Purse,

IN POINTS OF CERISE AND BLACK.

Three skeins of each color of middle-sized purse-silk, and " Penelope " crochet-needle, No. 4½, are required.

These purses are coming very much into use, and most gentlemen like them very much. The manner in which they are worked makes one end of the purse one color, and the other another, the two colors meeting in the centre in points. The two colors are convenient for distinguishing at which end the gold or silver is placed.

Make a chain of 112 stitches with black, draw the cerise silk through the black loop on the needle, and make 17 chain with it.

1st row.—Turn, miss 4 loops of the chain, work a long stitch into the 5th, * make 1 chain, miss 1 loop, work a long stitch in the next, repeat from * five times, make 1 chain, miss 1 loop, take up the silk and insert the needle in the next, draw the silk through, then take up the black silk and draw it through the 2 loops on the needle, and finish the stitch ; * make 1 chain, miss 1 loop, make a long stitch into the next ; repeat from * to the end of the row with black.

2d row.—Turn, make 4 chain, work 1 long stitch into the hole formed by the chain-stitch, make 1 chain, and repeat into every hole until within 8 holes of the cerise in last row, take the cerise silk and hold it along the top of the row, take up the black silk on the needle, draw it through the hole. Finish this stitch and the row with cerise.

3d row.—Turn, make 4 chain, work a long stitch into the first hole, make 1 chain and repeat, working 7 long stitches beyond the cerise in last row, and joining to the black as before in the 8th ; finish the row with black. Continue to work in this way, carrying the cerise 8 stitches farther on in each row until only 8 of black remain ; then decrease the cerise stitches, and increase the black in the same proportion. Repeat this until two perfect points of each are done. The purse will then be wide enough. It must be crocheted together, by working * a stitch of double crochet into the first hole on each side together, make 1 chain, repeat from * till 20 holes are joined.

For the mouth of the purse, work 2 stitches of double crochet into each of the next 23 holes on the side towards you ; work in the same way into the 23 corresponding holes on the other side, join the other end in the same way as the first, stretch it, and sew up the ends.

Tassels made of the same silk are very pretty.

7

Very Elegant Crochet Pattern,

IN CIRCLES, SUITABLE FOR LARGE COUVREPIED, QUILT, OR ANTIMACASSAR,
OR A SINGLE CIRCLE FOR A D'OYLEY OR PINCUSHION.

The object in designing this pattern is to introduce as many different stitches in crochet as can be placed in one pattern. Light quilts done in these sort of patterns are particularly fashionable just now; they are lined with silk or satin, according to the furniture of the room they are intended for.

For a quilt, six dozen of cotton, No. 12, and "Penelope" crochet-needle, No. 5, are required.

Fig. 77.

1*st round.*—Make a chain of 8 stitches and unite it.

2*d round.*—Work into the circle 16 stitches of double crochet.

3*d round.*—Work a stitch of double crochet over the 1st in last round, taking the front part of the loop, make 4 chain, miss 1 loop, and repeat; unite it to 1st of double crochet by a stitch of single crochet.

4*th round.*—Work into the back loops of 2d round, make 4 chain, work a long stitch into every loop, make 1 chain between each; at the end unite by a stitch of single crochet to the 3d stitch of 4 chain.

5th round.—Make a chain of 18 stitches, turn, and work into the 4th from the needle 1 long stitch, * make 1 chain, miss 1 loop, work a long stitch into the next, repeat from * three times; make 1 chain, miss 1 loop and work a stitch of single crochet into the next. Work into the hole formed by the 1 chain just missed, 2 stitches of double crochet, work 2 stitches of double crochet into each hole, between the long stitches till you come to the 3 chain left at the top, work 5 stitches of double crochet into these and 2 into each hole down the other side of leaf. Work 3 stitches of double crochet into the hole of the bottom, into which 2 have been already worked, * make 4 chain, miss 1 loop, work a stitch of double crochet into the front loop of next, repeat from * all round the leaf; unite by a stitch of single crochet to 1st of double crochet, make 2 chain, work into the back part of loops of double crochet round the centre of leaf, 10 long stitches into successive loops, make 2 long stitches into each of the next 5 loops, and 1 into each of the next 10 loops, make 1 chain, and unite by a stitch of single crochet to the 1st of 2 chain; work a stitch of double crochet into the next loop, * make 5 chain, miss 1 loop, work a stitch of double crochet into the next, taking both front and back loops up, repeat from * 16 times, unite by a stitch of single crochet to 1st of double crochet, work 2 stitches of single crochet into the 1st 2 loops of 18 chain, made at the beginning of the leaf.

This completes one leaf.

Work 7 stitches of single crochet into successive loops, beginning in the same loop as last of single crochet in 4th round.

Work 5 more leaves in the same manner. In working the last row of 2d leaf, unite it to the 1st in the 3d loop of 5 chain in the following manner: after making 2 chain, work a stitch of single crochet into the 3d chain of corresponding loop in 1st leaf, making 2 chain, and continue; join each leaf in the same way, and the 6th to the 5th and 1st.

6th round.—Work into the centre of 3d loop of 5 chain in first leaf, counting from the loop, next to that joined to second leaf, 9 extra-long stitches ; work a stitch of single crochet into the 1st extra long stitch, make 1 chain; work in the same way into the corresponding loop of second leaf, make 6 chain ; work 1 long stitch into the centre loop of next 5 chain, make 5 chain, miss the next, and work a stitch of double crochet into the centre loop of next 5 chain ; make 5 chain, miss 1 loop of 5 chain ; work 1 long stitch into the centre loop of next, make 6 chain, and repeat from the beginning of the round ; at the end unite by working a stitch of single crochet into the one that unites the 9 extra-long stitches.

7th round.—Work a stitch of double crochet into each loop except those of the extra-long stitches.

8th round.—Make 3 chain, work into the 1st loop 8 extra-long stitches ; unite to the 1st by a stitch of single crochet, make 3 chain ; work 13 stitches of single crochet into successive loops, and repeat from the beginning of the round.

9th round.—Work a stitch of double crochet into the 1st of 3 chain, make 8 chain, miss 1 loop, work 1 long stitch into the next, make 5 chain, work 1 long stitch into the top of 1st extra-long stitch, make 5 chain, work a long stitch into the stitch uniting the extra-long stitches ; make 5 chain ; work another long stitch into the same place, make 5 chain, work 1 long stitch into the top of last extra-long stitch, make 5 chain, work a long stitch into the centre of same extra-long stitch, make 5 chain, work 1 long stitch into the same as the 8 extra-long stitches, miss 3 loops of last round, work 7 stitches of single crochet into successive loops, repeat from the beginning of the round, work 1 long stitch, and 5 chain instead of 8 chain.

10th round.—Work into the 1st loop of chain 3 stitches of double crochet, * work into the centre loop of next 5 chain 3 long stitches, make 5 chain, work a stitch of single crochet into the top of last long stitch, work 2 more long stitches into the same loop as the 3; repeat from * once, work 4 long stitches into the next, make 3 loops of 5 chain, working a stitch of single crochet into the top of the 4th long stitch after each; work 3 more long stitches into the same place as the 4, work 3 loops to correspond with them on the other side of the point. In working the second point, unite it to the first in the centre of 1st loop of 5 chain. There will be 12 of these points; the last must be united on both sides. This completes the circle. When the circles are all united, it will be found that some small pattern is wanted to fill up the space; nothing can be better than the centre of this circle.

Sprigs and Edging for Honiton Lace.

Having referred in the chapter upon Lace Work to this chapter for the crochet sprigs to be used in making imitation Honiton lace, a few are here given.

When worked, they must be carefully sewed to the net foundation with fine thread. The net or muslin must be tacked to dark glazed paper cut in the required shape, the sprigs or edging basted to the muslin, not through the paper; then removed from the paper and sewed to the muslin.

Honiton Sprigs.—No. 1.

[Cotton, No. 50.—Needle No. 24, for this and all succeeding Honiton Lace.]

This pattern (Fig. 78) is particularly suitable for a veil or fall. It forms the lower border, and the upper part may be ornamented with any sprigs your taste may suggest as suitable; only the first row should not be very light or small. Each pattern is complete in itself, as it is engraved; and when you wish to form many into the border of a veil or Bertha, lay them in their proper places; and unite them with your needle and thread where they happen to touch. The pear edging is sewed on when the article is finished.

Begin with the upper of the two bars in the open work of the large leaf, where it is marked *a*, 45 Ch., miss 4, Dc. on 5th, + 3 Ch., miss 3, Dc. on 4th + 9 times; 3 Ch., slip 1, work up the other side of the 45 Ch., ‖ 3 Ch., Dc. on centre of the 3 missed in the last row, ‖ 8 times; 3 Ch., Sc. on 4th, slip 4, 7 Ch., now form the lowest row of open hem, Dc. on the last of the 4 slip, ⊕ 3 Ch., miss 3, Dc. on 4th, ⊕ 8 times; 3 Ch., miss 3, Sc. on 4th, slip 4. This completes the open-work: work round in Dc., working two into every one round the point. The edge is worked as follows: + 1 Sc., 1 Dc., 1 Tc., 2 long Tc., 1 Tc., 1 Dc., 1 Sc., 1 slip, + repeat all round the leaf, working two stitches into one at the point. STEM.—20 Ch.

STAR FLOWER.—22 Ch., slip in 13th for loop, Sc. all round, ‖ 8 Ch., 7 slip, Sc. all round, 1 slip on loop, ‖ 5 times; 12 Sc. on Ch.
12 Ch. for stem.

LEAF, No. 1. —22 Ch., miss 3, Dc. on 4th, ⊕ 2 Ch., miss 2, Dc. on 3d, ⊕ twice, 2 Ch. 1 Sc. 1 slip. Slip 1 round, slip on stem : for the loops, + 11 Ch., miss 2, Dc. through 3d, + 4 times, 11 Ch. slip, work round in Sc., missing every 12th. 8 Sc. on stem.
Repeat leaf, 12 Ch., for main stem.

LEAF, No. 2.—26 Ch., 1 Dc. on 23d, + 3 Ch., Tc. on 4th, + repeat, 3 Ch. Dc, in 4th, 3 Ch., Sc. in 4th, slip 1. Work up the other side (leaving 5 Ch. for stem), 2 Ch., Dc. on 3d, ‖ 3 Ch., Tc. on 4th, ‖ 3 times, taking care that the middle one of the three missed in the last row is now taken up; 3 Ch. slip at the

Fig. 78.

point, and slip-stitch down the centre, ⊕ 1 Sc., 2 Dc., 2 Tc., 1 long Tc., 1 Tc., 1 Dc., 1 slip ⊕ repeat; and again for the point working 2 in 1, repeat also twice for the other side of the leaf, but reversing the directions (1 slip, 1 Dc., etc.), 5 Sc. on stem.   Or the leaf, No. 1, may be repeated.

Repeat 1st leaf, with 12 Ch., instead of 8, for stem.   Then opposite 2d leaf, + 18 Ch., slip 11 for small leaf, and work round in Sc., leaving 6 Ch. for stem.   + Repeat this last leaf, forming part of the flower.   1 Ch., 11 slip, 5 Sc. 5 Ch., for the short bar to connect the two leaves, join to the corresponding side of the last leaf; work back in Sc., 4 Sc. on leaf, 9 Ch. (for long bar), join to point of last leaf, work back in Sc. and down the other side of the leaf, 6 Sc. on Ch.   Small leaf opposite 1st 6 Sc. on Ch., and 6 on the main stem.

SMALL OPEN LEAF.—16 Ch. join into a loop; work round in Dc., except the first and last stitches, which must be Sc.; finish with slip-stitch.

12 Sc. on Ch.; repeat star flower; 12 Sc. on Ch.; repeat small open leaf, 14 Sc. on Ch.; fasten off.

No. 2.—Sprig.

22 Ch. (viz. 6 for main stem, 8 for flower stem, 8 for flower); work back on the last 8, 1 Sc., 1 Dc., 3 Tc., 1 Dc., 1 slip; 8 Ch.; turn on the wrong side, and do 9 Ch.; join to the point of the leaf, and work back in Sc., then on the 8, as before; and 8 Sc. on stem; 8 Ch. for stem.

ROSE LEAF.—26 Ch., 1 slip, + 2 Ch., Dc., on 3d, + twice, 13 Ch., slip 1, ⊕ 2 Ch., Dc. on 3d ⊕ twice, ∴ 8 Ch. slip 1, 2 Ch., Dc. in 3d, 2 Ch., Dc. in 3d, ∴ repeat, Dc. in 6th of 13 Ch., 2 Ch., Dc. in 3d, 2 Ch., Dc. in 3d, 8 Ch., slip 1, 2 Ch., Dc. in 3d, 2 Ch., Dc. in 3d., Dc. in the 9th of the 16th; 2 Ch. Sc. on 6th of

Fig. 79.

the 16.   Slip-stitch on the 5th, leaving 4 for the stem; five open veinings are thus formed, which are worked round as follows:

1st.   Work up the side, to the point in Dc., working two stitches in one every other time.   Down the other side work plainly in Dc., and join to the centre open hem, by taking a slip-stich through the centre of the five chain that are between the two fibres.

2d.   Work as the first; but, before twisting the thread round the needle for the first five stitches, pass the hook through the edge of each of the last five, thus connecting them together.

3d.   All round in Dc., working two stitches in one round the point.

4th.   In Dc., working only one stitch in each on the first side, and two in every alternate of the second.

5th.   As 4th, joining the first 5 stitches as I have already directed for the 21.   4 Sc. on the stem-completes this beautiful leaf.

STEM.—10 Ch.

LARGE FLOWER.—15 Ch., work back, 1 slip, 1 Sc., 2 Dc. in one chain, 8 Tc., 1 Dc., 1 Sc., 1 slip; 1 Ch. Turn the work on the wrong side. 5 Ch. for bar, join to the eighth of opposite side; turn on the right side; slip on 5 Ch., 8 Ch.; turn on the wrong side. 9 Ch., slip-stitch on the 3d of the 5, 9 Ch., join to point of the opposite side, turn back. Sc. on the 18 Ch., missing the slip-stitch in the centre. Work down the 15 chain, as the first 15 were done; but to give the graceful form to the flower the 7th and 9th stitches must be contracted; thus—

(Work a Tc. stitch until you have only two loops on the needle, and, without finishing it, work the next stitch, drawing the cotton through three loops at once at last; thus, whilst you have worked two stitches on the chain, you have worked but one edge. Work the remainder as usual, and finish with a slip-stitch.)

10 Sc. on Ch. Repeat rose leaf, 8 Sc. on Ch.

SMALL ROSE LEAF.—16 Ch., slip 1, + 2 Ch., Dc. on 3d, + twice, ⊕ 8 Ch. to 1, 2 Ch., Dc. on 3d, 2 Ch., Dc. on 3d, ⊕ repeat, Dc. in 9th of the 16. 2 ., miss 2. Sc. in 6th, slip in 5th, leaving 4 for the stem. Work round these things like the first, third, and fourth of the large leaf, and finish the sprig with Sc. on the stalk.

No. 3.—Sprig.

You will find, in working this sprig from the directions I am about to give, that you will make one exactly reversing the appearance presented in the engraving; that is, the stem and flower will lean in the contrary direction, the long leaf will be on the lower, and the three small ones on the upper, side. Of this I must endeavor to give you an explanation. In order to preserve uniformity in many articles, it is desirable to be able to reverse patterns; as, for instance, in the opposite corners of collars and Berthas; and nothing can be more simple, when you are once taught how to do it.

Having worked a sprig according to the directions, lay it on a piece of colored paper, with the wrong side uppermost, and draw a pattern of it, marking the figures in their proper places. With the help of the written directions in forming the different leaves and flowers, you may reverse every pattern without trouble. To make it, however, as intelligible as possible, I shall give you the directions for the reverse of this sprig, which I have selected for the experiment on account of its simplicity. The flower is worked the same in both patterns.

30 Ch., 24 Sc. on Ch., leaving 5 Ch. for the stem. On the other side of the chain work 4 Sc., 10 Dc., 7 Tc., 1 Dc., 1 Sc., 1 slip. Turn the work on the wrong side, + 9 Ch., miss 4, Sc. through 5th, + 3 times, 7 Ch., miss 3, Sc. through 4th; 5 Ch., slip-stitch through the 1st of the leaf. Turn the work on the right side, and work the five loops in Sc., working only the chain-stitches; then slip-stitch along the other edge of the leaf, which completes it.

24 Ch. for stem.

FLOWER.—28 Ch.; form into a loop and work round in Sc.; 9 Ch., fasten with a slip-stitch in the centre of the circle (*a*), slip round to (*b*), 4 Ch., slip in 5th of 9, 4 Ch., join to the quarter of the round at (*c*), turn on the wrong side, and slip to stem, + 7 Ch., miss 3, Dc. through 4th, + 6 times; 7 Ch., miss 3, slip through the stem, and work round in Sc., missing every Dc. stitch.

8 Sc. on stem.

CLOSE LEAF.—12 Ch., 11 slip, on each side of which work 1 Sc., 2 Dc., 5 Tc., 2 Dc. 1 Sc., with 1 slip at the point.

+ 8 Sc. on stem, leaf, + repeat, and work 5 Sc. on the 5 chain to complete it.

104   LADIES' GUIDE TO NEEDLEWORK.

In reversing this pattern, make 5 Ch. for stem, then three leaves with 8 Ch.
after each, the flower, and 24 Sc. on the three-times-eight chain-stitches. A little
thought will be required for the large leaf, which may be worked thus : Large
leaf reversed, 25 Ch., 24 slip on ditto ; on the upper edge work Sc.; on the lower
1 slip, 1 Sc., 1 Dc., 7 Tc., 10 Dc., 3 Sc., 1 slip. Turn the work on the wrong
side, 5 Ch., miss 3, Sc. through 4th, 7 Ch., miss 3, Sc. through 4th, + 9 Ch.,
miss 4, Sc. through 5th, + 3 times, taking the last stitch through the point of the
leaf ; turn on the right side, and work in Sc.
A little practice will enable you to reverse your patterns without any difficulty.

No. 4.—Sprig.

This sprig is done in three pieces. The two heavy parts, which form nearly
the entire edge [marked respectively twenty and fourteen], are done first, and in
working the flower they are to be fastened on in their proper places. I must
therefore begin with directions for making these.
1st PIECE.—20 Ch., miss 1, 1 Dc. and 1 Tc. in the 2d, 3 Tc. in 3d, 2 Tc. in
4th, 5th, 6th, 7th, 8th, Tc. the remainder, and draw the thread through the last
loop to fasten off.
2d PIECE.—34 Ch., miss 20, Tc. 2, then + 2 Tc. in 1 Ch. + 8 times. 3 Tc.
in 1, 1 Tc., 1 Dc. in 10 slip ; on the other side of the chain, 6 Ch., 1 Sc., 4 Dc.
on chain, 2 Dc., 1 Sc., 2 slip on the 1st chain. 8 chain. 1 Sc., 6 Dc. on chain,
2 Dc., 1 Sc. on 1st Ch., slip-stitch to the end, fasten off.
LARGE FLOWER (beginning with the calyx).—12 Ch., miss 5, Dc. on 6th, 2
Ch., Dc. on 3d, 2 Ch., slip on 3d. Up one side of the calyx, 1 slip, 2 Sc., 4 Dc.,
1 Sc., 1 slip. 30 Ch., join to the calyx, missing 1, and make the cross bars, thus :
Bar 3 Ch., join with slip-stitch in 3d to 30 Ch. 4 slip on 30, bar 7 Ch., join
to last but 4 of 30. 4 slip up 30, bar 7 Ch., join at the 4th from the last
bar. You have thus three bars in one direction, which must be crossed by three
bars in the contrary direction, catching up the first three where they happen
to cross. Work round the 30 thus : 1 slip, 2 Sc., Dc. all the rest but three.
2 Sc., 1 slip. Turn on the wrong side. 16 Ch., miss 3, slip on 4th, + * 4 slip
on last of chain, 16 Ch., miss 4, slip on 5th, + 5 times, 4 slip on the last chain,
12 Ch., miss 3, slip on calyx. Turn on the right side, and work two loops in Sc.
3d LOOP.—4 Sc., 2 Dc., 8 Ch. Small close leaf. as in Sprig 1st, but with 8
chain instead of 12. 8 chain for stem. 14 Ch., form into a loop, and work round
to the centre, 1 slip, 1 Sc., 3 Dc., 1 Sc., 1 slip. Small close leaf, then the remainder of the loop, as before. 8 slip on chain. Small close leaf opposite the
1st ; 8 slip on chain, then finish the loop of the flower with 3 Dc., 3 Sc.
4th LOOP.—3 Sc., 1 Dc., then with the next 3 Dc., join the short pieces of
work first done, 2 Dc., 3 Sc.
5th.—3 Sc., 3 Dc., join in the second separate piece, taking care to place it in the
proper position, with 3 Dc. stitches, 3 Sc.
6th and 7th LOOPS.—Sc., then the side of the calyx. 1 slip, 1 Sc., 4 Dc., 2
Sc., 1 slip, which completes the flower.
16 Ch., work back. 1 Sc., + 2 Dc. in 1 chain, + 4 times, 1 Dc., 9 chain. 1
Sc. in chain, 6 Dc. (contracting every alternate, as in Sprig 2), 1 Dc., 1 Tc. in the
next chain of the 16, 1 Dc. in next, 1 Sc. in next, 1 slip ; slip back on the last
3 stitches ; 6 Ch., work back, 1 slip, 1 Sc., 8 Dc., contracted, the last will come
on the 16 chain, 2 Sc., 1 slip, leaving 2 chain for the stem. 8 chain.

* In the engraving there are 20 chain marked, i. e. 4 slip on chain and 16 separate.

SHAMROCK.—21 Ch., join in 7th for a loop, and slip back 4 on the last 4; 11 chain, join to the stitch which made the loop, slip back 4 as before; 11 Ch.; join at the loop, and work round the trefoil in Sc., 6 Sc. on stem.

14 Ch. for stem; small close leaf, as in No. 1, 6 Ch. for stem.

DOUBLE LEAF.—14 Ch., miss 1, 1 Sc., 3 Dc., slip back on the last 3, and make 6 more chain; altogether the 20 marked—work 1 Sc., 4 Dc., 8 Tc., 2 Dc., 2 Sc., 2 slip.

6 Ch. for stem. Small close leaf of 8 Ch.

FLOWER.—21 Ch., miss 7, Long Tc. in 8th, + 2 Ch., Long Tc. in 3d, + twice; 2 Ch., Dc. in 3d, 2 Ch., slip in 3d; work round in Sc., with a slip-stitch first and last; 17 Ch., Sc. in top Long Tc. bar; 12 Ch., join with Sc. to the other end of the same Tc. bar; 17 Ch., join at the stem; work two loops, and 8 stitches of the 3d in Sc., 8 Ch., 3 small close leaves of 10 chain each, 8 Sc. on chain, and complete the loop.

SMALL CLOSE LEAF.—10 Sc. on the main stem, and a small close leaf of 12 chain; 10 Sc. on the chain, and repeat the Shamrock; Sc. on the stem, to the flower.

Complicated as this may appear, it is really very easy to work, especially if you keep a drawing of it before you whilst doing so. You may easily do this by drawing it on tracing paper, and putting the figures in their proper places, and you will be astonished to find how much it assists you. This sprig forms a beautiful edging. With the aid of the two separate pieces it is an edging; without them a sprig, which will serve for any purpose.

Edging.

One pattern of this edging consists of the flower which forms the border, with one large leaf and two small open ditto. Begin the stem at the point where it joins the large leaf of the preceding pattern, and make 18 chain, and 20 chain for the

SMALL OPEN LEAF.—Form these 20 into a loop, and work round 1 Sc., 8 Dc., 3 Dc., in 10th chain; 8 Dc., 1 Sc., 1 slip on the joining of the loop. 8 chain for the stem.

FLOWER.—20 chain for the centre loop, join, and work round in Sc. 5 chain; miss 3, Tc. in 4th; + 5 chain, miss 2, Tc. on 3d + 4 times; 5 chain, miss 3, slip on the stem; work round in Sc. Then the outer row of loops + 16 chain, miss 4, Sc. through 5th + 6 times; 16 chain, slip on the stem. Work round in Dc., 12 Sc. on chain.

LARGE LEAF.—18 chain, miss 5, Dc. on 6th; 2 chain, Tc. on 3d: 2 chain, Dc. on 3d; 2 chain, Sc. on 3d; 2 chain, slip on 3d. Work each of the seven petals 1 Sc., 1 Dc., 2 Tc., 1 Dc., 1 slip, which 6 stitches must be worked into 4 chain at the sides, and round the point at the top, where 3 Tc. must be worked, instead of 2.

8 Sc. on chain. Small open leaf, as before. 6 Sc. on chain.

This completes one sprig, and a number laid together will form an edging. For making up any article with this edging, the flower is to be laid so as to fall beyond the net to which the inner line of the flower is to be attached; and when the required number are laid in their proper positions and tacked on the net, connect them together by working all the scollops round in Sc.

This edging would look very well for a collar; but in order to form the corners, you must work two flowers, without any leaves, and with only short stems; put them in the proper places, and arrange the sprigs on each side, so that the pattern may appear uniform. The corners of a veil must be managed in the same way, if bordered all round with this edging, but I think that either No. 1 or No. 4 has a more elegant effect for the lower edge.

Every article, when completed, must be trimmed with the best pearl edging, laid on underneath, so that the little points alone are visible.

Raised Crochet.

Raised or ribbed crochet is worked in rows from right to left, according to the ordinary method; but the side of the work is reversed at every alternate row, as in plain crochet; hence it becomes the same as that description of work, with this exception, that the back or under stitch is always to be taken; it has, therefore, a ribbed or raised appearance, and is rendered thicker and closer, and of a more elastic texture.

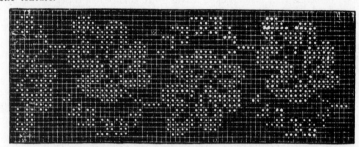

Fig. 80.

The annexed design is well adapted for working in raised crochet. The color forming the pattern should only be introduced when necessary, and should not be carried on through the ground, as in plain double crochet; therefore, the same thread must be taken up and dropped, as the form of the pattern may require—a process by no means difficult. When necessary, however, the idle wool should be carried through the stitches of that in use, and not left loose at the back.

The pattern here given is intended to be worked in stripes; these are afterwards to be sewn together. It is very handsome for quilts, couvrepieds, &c. The colors may be varied, thus—first stripe, white, with the pattern in scarlet; the second, scarlet, with the pattern in white. Shaded wools may be used for the pattern on a plain ground.

Table-Cover in Raised Crochet.

Commence with a chain of black. Work one row in two stitches of black and two of scarlet alternately. Then one row of scarlet and one row of black; the latter forms the ground of the border—the pattern of which is in four shades of gold color, two rows of each, commencing with the darkest. One plain row of black and one of scarlet finish the border.

Crochet one plain row of white, then one plain row of blue; the latter forms the ground of the centre. The colors of the pine pattern are as follows:

1st row—middle scarlet.
2d row—light scarlet.
3d row—three stitches drab, two black, three drab.
4th row—three stitches white, two black, three white.

5th row—three stitches gold color, two lilac, three gold color.
6th row—three stitches yellow, two lilac, three yellow.
7th row—three stitches middle scarlet, two black, three middle scarlet.

Fig. 81.

8th row—three stitches light scarlet, two black, three light scarlet.
9th row—drab.
10th row—white.

Fig. 82.—BORDER PATTERN FOR SQUARE.

Border Pattern for a Square in Raised Crochet.

This pattern may be employed for a tidy, sofa pillow, mat, carpet, cradle or bed quilt, carriage wrapper, d'oyley, and a variety of other purposes where a border on each side may be required. It may be worked either in plain double crochet or in raised crochet. A different material, together with a different sized needle, are the only requisites to adapt it to any of the above purposes. Thus,—

For a sofa pillow, eight-thread zephyr fleecy; for a tidy, three-thread fleecy; for a window-mat, eight-thread common fleecy; for a flower-mat, German or English wool; for a cradle-quilt, eight-thread zephyr fleecy; for a bed-quilt, six-thread fleecy; for a d'oyley, rather fine knitting cottons. The size of the article, however, must in the first instance be determined, and the number of stitches counted, so as to bring in the pattern as suited to that size. The simplest coloring will be the most effective—a plain ground, with the pattern in any bright color.

Work-Basket in Crochet.

Materials: cardboard; colored silk; gray and brown knitting cotton; yellow floss; cord and tassels to match silk. Steel crochet hook.

Make a chain of 116 stitches with gray cotton.

1st row.—Put the cotton over the hook, one single into the next stitch; repeat, keeping all the stitches on the hook; coming back, pull through two loops together.

2d row.—The same as first, working the single by taking up the two perpendicular loops of last row.

3d row.—The same as last.

4th row.—With brown cotton, work in treble crochet, taking up the two perpendicular loops of last row; coming back, draw through each loop.

5th row.—With gray cotton, put the hook through the centre of perpendicular loops of last row, draw up a loop; repeat; coming back, with brown, pull through each loop.

6th row.—The same as last; coming back, draw through each loop with yellow floss.

7th row.—The same as fifth row, putting the cotton over the hook before working each stitch; coming back, pull through two loops together.

8th, 9th, 10th, 11th, 12th, 13th, 14th, 15th, 16th rows.—Like the first, with gray cotton.

17th, 18th, 19th, 20th rows.—The same as 4th, 5th, 6th, and 7th rows.

21st, 22d, 23d rows.—The same as 1st, 2d, and 3d rows.

The border edge is made as follows:

Make a chain sufficiently long to go round the top, and lower edges of the work just finished. Work a row of treble crochet with the brown cotton; coming back, pull through each loop with yellow floss, on each side of this work with gray cotton; one double in the first, five treble in the next; take out the hook, put it through the top loop of first double, put it again through the loop from which it was withdrawn, one double in the next stitch of brown. Repeat on both sides for the length required.

The handle is made in the same way as just described for the trimming, and is then twisted together (see No. 6). It is laid over a strip of cardboard covered with silk.

An oval piece of cardboard covered with silk forms the bottom of the basket.
The sides as far as the crochet require a foundation of cardboard, lined with silk ;
and a silk top with slide is sewn to the upper edge of the silk lining.

Fig. 83.—WORK-BASKET IN CROCHET.

CHAPTER X.

NETTING.

The age of netting is of great antiquity, having been practised from the earliest ages alike by the most refined and the most uncivilized nations. In the fourth chapter of St. Matthew, twenty-first verse, we read of our Saviour's disciples as " mending their nets;" it is, therefore, probable that the art has been known for at least two thousand years.

The method of teaching it by explanation is not easy, nor would Dr. Johnson's definition of it induce many young ladies to learn netting. He describes it as " a complicated concatenation of rectangular angles." But I will endeavor to give a more simple explanation.

The implements necessary for this branch of elegant needlework are a netting needle and a mesh. The material may be any strong thread, silk, cotton, linen, or wool. The variety of stitches is very great.

To make the plain netting stitch, thread a netting needle, taking care to tie the end of the thread or silk firmly through the hole in it, to prevent its slipping ; then take a piece of string or ribbon, rather more than a yard and a half, join the ends and place it over the foot; tie the end of the thread to that part of the ribbon that reaches the hand; take a round mesh; pass the thread over the mesh, on to the second finger of left hand under the mesh in front of the ribbon, and hold it back with the thumb of the left hand ; insert the netting needle between the loop on second finger and under the string, catch back the thread with the little finger; draw the needle through and let off the thread from the middle finger, and then off the little finger; draw the thread close up to the mesh ; this will make a knot. Repeat this till about forty stitches are done, slip out the mesh, turn the row just done, and net in the same way, only putting the needle into the hole formed by each stitch, instead of under the string ; net a number of rows, until the netting looks quite even, that is, all the stitches of the same length and the knots exactly opposite to each other.

Beginners are very apt to make long stitches, and it is very troublesome to unpick them, but it must be done. Take a pointed needle and gradually loosen the knot ; then pass the needle back through the loop ; this wi'l undo it. A whole piece of netting would be spoiled by one long stitch.

Numbers of very pretty things can be made in netting, such as tidies, curtains, purses and other articles.

Grecian Netting.

This should be worked in fine silk, and with two meshes, one much larger than the other, as Nos. 7 and 14. One plain row is to be netted with the large mesh, the next row with the small one. The silk is twisted round the finger, as in plain netting, and the needle must pass through the finger loop into the first stitch, and then to the second. Then let the second be drawn through the first, and the first through the second, finishing the stitch by releasing the fingers and pulling the thread tight. The next stitch is a small loop, that appears to cross the stitches twisted together. This trio of stitches forms the pattern and is repeated alternately until the work is completed.

Honeycomb Netting, for a Purse.

The materials required are four skeins of medium-sized purse-silk, steel mesh, No. 16, and a steel netting-needle.

Make a strong foundation of the plain netting-stitch first described, in an even number.

1st row.—Plain netting, passing the silk twice round the mesh.

2d row.—With the silk once round the mesh half twist the second stitch, and then net it; net the first stitch plain, next the fourth stitch the same as second, and the third stitch the same as first; repeat in this manner to the end of the row.

3d row.—Plain netting, with the silk twice round the mesh.

4th row.—Same as second; repeat these alternately; when a sufficient width is done for the purse, net together one-third of the length at each end, sew up the mouth, and put it on a stretcher. This will make the netting look more even. Crochet round the mouth of the purse, one stitch of double crochet into each loop.

Spotted Netting, for Purses.

Use the same needle and mesh as in the honey-comb netting. Make a foundation that will divide by seven.

1st and 2d rows.—Plain netting.

3d row.—Net 7 stitches, pass the silk round the mesh, and the needle through below the knot in the second row, but without netting it. This is between the stitch first netted and the one next to be done. Repeat to the end of the row.

4th row.—Net six stitches; then the loop-stitch with the seventh; repeat.

This spotting can be done in a variety of simple forms. It looks very pretty with one spot in the first place, as just described, then three spots, one beyond each side, then one in the middle of the three.

To close a purse in netting, after picking out the knots from the foundation, fasten the silk with a weaver's knot to the end of the silk at the beginning, hold the two sides of the purse, net a stitch into the first loop of the side farthest from you, then a stitch into the first loop of the side nearest, and so on alternately until one-third of the length is closed; then, without cutting off the silk, crochet into each loop of one-third, net the remainder together, and crochet the other side of the mouth.

For a clasped purse, the netting must be narrowed by taking up two loops in every third row, till about one-fourth the width commenced, and widened in the same way returning, by doubling one loop on every third row. The two sides must then be closed by netting them together, and the ends sewed to the clasp.

Diamond Netting.

This kind of netting is at once simple and pretty. It is done by making every other stitch a loop-stitch, in order to effect which the silk must be put twice round the mesh, instead of once, as in plain netting.

Treble diamond netting is similar, but the process is rather more difficult. After netting three plain rows to commence the work, the first row is to be composed of one loop-stitch, and three plain stitches, until the row is finished; then, in working the second row, commence with the plain stitch, follow with a loop, take two plain stitches, and repeat as before. For the third row, begin with two plain stitches, make a loop, a plain stitch, two loops and a plain stitch alternating to the end of the row. For the fourth row, net three plain stitches, a loop-stitch, and repeat.

Diamond Netted Curtain, with Scalloped Border.

Eight dozen reels of netting-cotton, No. 8, will be required, and two steel meshes, Nos. 8 and 11.

The number of stitches for the foundation must be calculated according to the length required for the curtains.

Fig. 84.

Net four rows plain, on mesh No. 8.

5th row.—On mesh No. 11, net one stitch; net the second, passing the cotton round the mesh; repeat.

6th row.—Plain netting, drawing up the short stitch half way, so as to make it even with the other.

Repeat the fifth and sixth rows until twenty-four are done, then net four plain rows on the No. 8 mesh.

29th row.—Plain netting on mesh No. 8.

30th row.—Net fifteen stitches, pass the cotton twice round the mesh; repeat.

31st row.—Net till you come to the loop-stitch, pass the needle under it, then net it, pass the cotton round the mesh, under the last netted stitch, and net the next.

32d row.—Net thirteen stitches, make a loop by passing the cotton twice round, net two stitches, make a loop, and repeat.

33d row.—Net thirteen, pass the needle under the loop, then net it: pass the cotton over the mesh, under the last loop, net two stitches, pass the cotton under the loop, net it, pass the cotton over the mesh, under the loop, net the next stitch, and repeat.

34th and *35th rows.*—The same, making three loops instead of two.

35th row.—Same as 32d.

Repeat from 29th row twice. The diamond of holes must be made to come in centre of plain stitches in 29th row.

Repeat from 1st row until the curtain is wide enough.

For the scalloped edging, make a foundation of a yard at a time, as it is easily joined, and a long foundation is troublesome for so few rows. Three different sized meshes will be required—an ivory one, three-quarters of an inch wide, and a steel mesh each of Nos. 13 and 17.

1st row.—On the wide mesh knit sixteen stitches into each loop.

2d row.—Net one plain stitch into each loop with mesh No. 13.

3d row.—With the smallest mesh pass the thread twice round the mesh, net two plain stitches in the next loop ; repeat to the end of the row.

4th row.—With mesh No. 13 net the long stitches only, leaving the increased stitches without netting; net two plain rows on No. 13 mesh ; this completes the scallop.

In netting with beads, the beads must be fastened with the knot. Patterns can easily be made by following the plan of the knotting as if it were a square of canvas. String all the beads required upon the silk before commencing to net.

A Novel Net for the Hair.

The materials in this net would puzzle many of those who have admired its effect, being simply cucumber seeds mixed with beads. The one from which this description is taken was made of dark blue crochet silk, blue and gold beads, and cucumber seeds that were similar to carved wood in appearance. But any color may be used to suit the wearer. In many dresses for fancy balls, tableaux, or private theatricals, a net over the hair is very effective, although they are now but little worn. Yet hair-nets, like many other fashions, appear and disappear, and are always likely to be worn, being becoming to most faces, and covering many deficiencies in the quantity or arrangement of the hair.

The beads used must match the seeds in size. Three strings of gold beads, ten of blue, and four ounces of cucumber seeds, are required. The beads must be threaded, with the thin end first pierced by the needle, which must pass through the inside of the seed to the thick end.

Select a needle which will pass easily through the beads, and use either silk or linen thread, as strong as the needle will hold. Silk to match the beads in color is the best.

Make a knot in the silk, and thread on twenty-four seeds at the thin end, and as near the point as possible without splitting. Join these into a ring by tying the thread, and run your needle through the thick end of the first seed, ready to begin the second row.

Be careful to use needlesful of thread about a yard long, and to fasten off only when you have to take a fresh one, as the thread passing from one point to the other of the seed is sufficiently invisible.

2d row.—The thread being run through the thick part of one of the twenty-four seeds, thread on two new seeds, then another of the twenty-four, then two more, and so on, making forty-eight seeds on the second row. Bring the thread through the thick part of one for the next row. This direction must be followed for the beginning of every new row.

3d row.—Two new seeds, then through one of the last row, three blue beads, and through another of the last row; repeat.

The next eight rows may be done in the same way, putting two more blue beads on in each place every new row, so that the fourth row will have five, the fifth row seven, the sixth row nine, and the eleventh nineteen beads on each division, while

8

the seeds, being arranged with the thin points of two new seeds between the thick points of two of the last row, present the appearance of heads of corn.

The twelfth row is to be worked like the preceding; but thread on two seeds in the centre of each line of beads, of which you will add one only. You will thus have two lines of ten beads each, instead of a single line of twenty-one.

13th row.—The thread being brought through the thick part of the seed, as usual, put on one bead, then the other seed, four beads, one gold, four blue, three seeds, four blue beads, one gold, four blue, and through the thick part of the next to the last row; repeat.

14th row.—Like the last, thread a blue bead between each two of the three seeds, and adding a blue bead on one side of the gold, if you find it is necessary to fit the head.

In the next row you may increase on each side of the gold; and so you may go on, gradually increasing the size by adding blue beads, until it is large enough for the head, which must, of course, principally depend upon whether it is designed to cover the back hair only, or to come forward. By the exercise of a little ingenuity, tassels may be made to correspond, which, with the aid of hairpins, will keep the net in place. If only intended to cover the coil at the back, an elastic band may be run in.

CHAPTER XI.

TRANSFERRING.

Transferring, a few years ago, applied only to one kind of work, that of taking the embroidery from old and wornout muslin or lace and putting it on new material. But new transfer work has been introduced into the fancy stores, which will be described later in this chapter.

The original transfer work will probably be done as long as muslin or lace embroidery exists, as the fine beautiful work done in France and Ireland will bear cutting again and again, never wearing out when the material upon which it is embroidered is long past service.

To transfer embroidery, all the work had better not be cut at once, as the tiny sprigs, leaves or flowers are apt to be lost if many are loosened from their foundation at once. The muslin or net upon which they are to be placed should be first cut into the shape required, and pinned with fine pins to a stiff paper. Then the work should be cut out and basted to the muslin, with one stitch only for each piece, the stitch not passing through the paper. When the pattern is completed, very fine thread must be threaded in a fine cambric needle, and the work sewed down in firm, but close, fine stitches on the wrong side, first removing the muslin from the paper. When this is done, the edges of the work must be fastened down with tiny invisible stitches on the right side. The muslin edge must be carefully cut away with fine embroidery scissors, after the embroidered edge is sewed down. No edge but buttonhole stitch will look well. When there are tendrils and fine lines in the transferred work, it is better to cut them off and embroider the spaces they were intended to fill, as they are so fine that the neatest sewing will not prevent their appearing clumsy.

Large pieces of French embroidery or India muslin can be used again for smaller articles, such as handkerchief corners or neckties, when utterly useless on the original foundation.

Transfer work is extensively used for fine lace neckties and scarfs, exquisite little sprigs, leaves, flowers, stars and other designs being carefully and neatly sewed to the broad end of the lace, and giving it a beautiful finish.

Japanese Transfer Work

can be obtained in all the fancy stores, and is very popular for every kind of cloth embroidery, table-cloth borderings, corners, slippers, chair-covers, and lambrequins.

It is always made in grotesque figures when any attempt at imitating animals or human figures is made, but some of the birds and flowers are very beautiful.

It comes in colored and black cloth, ornamented with embroidery in vivid colors, and gummed down upon a thin paper. The work of transferring is very easy.

The pattern is basted down upon the cloth to be ornamented, and then fastened to it with a long but close buttonhole or satin-stitch in silk, gold color being usually the most effective. The stitches are taken through the paper to which the patterns are gummed, and loosen it so that it tears off easily after the work is done. Slippers done in Japanese transfer work have largely superseded the old-fashioned ones in canvas work, and the taste inclines to the most grotesque designs, demons and distorted animals being in great demand.

Another kind of transfer work, somewhat resembling cretonne work, consists of cutting the large groups of flowers or birds from the old-fashioned brocaded silk, and transferring them to cloth, silk, or velvet, for such articles as would otherwise be embroidered. I have seen an apron of black silk with a border cut from an old-fashioned brocade, that appeared like the heaviest silk embroidery. The brocade was a rich wine color, and the pattern was sewed to the black silk by satin stitch of the exact shade in tiny, even stitches. The same hands had made a portfolio on black velvet, with the figures cut from variegated damask, every stitch of the transferring—close satin-stitch—matching exactly the edge of the damask. The designs, a wreath of flowers on one side and a group on the other, were of great beauty, and appeared to be embroidered on the velvet.

A pretty kind of transfer work, very saleable at a fancy fair, is made by purchasing the bright-colored French and German pictures now so extensively sold, and gumming them upon perforated card, to be made into fancy articles. When the card is lined, bound, and made up, these little bright-colored pictures are quite as effective as the work usually wrought upon this material, and the amount of time and labor bestowed is materially lessened.

A pretty patchwork can be made in transfer work, by cutting out the bright-colored figures in calico and sewing them down upon a white ground, or on plain cambric in any neutral tint. Small pieces left from larger work can be made available in this way, and are very effective.

The figures must be carefully cut with very sharp scissors, care being taken to leave a narrow margin all round; this margin must be turned down on the wrong side; the figure must then be basted upon the plain cambric and hemmed down. If the figures are all taken from one piece of goods, the effect is merely the same as if they were printed upon the plain material, but when they are varied in shape and color, a very odd and brilliant quilt can be made. A high-colored palm leaf in one block, a bird in a second, a group of flowers in a third, a star in a fourth, and so on, without any attempt at regularity, makes the prettiest combination, and the variety of color now procurable in plain French cambric will give great variety in the groundwork. As there is a great deal of work in this, it is best to procure the French calico, the colors being more brilliant and durable than in other manufactures.

A work-basket has been shown me in this work that was very handsome. The groundwork was of soft grey French cambric, and upon each piece was sewed a pattern cut from French chintz, every piece having a different figure. The foundation of the basket was of stiff pasteboard. The bottom piece was a perfect octagon, and the sides matching each division of the octagon at the base, widened one-third at the top to make the basket. Each piece of pasteboard was covered with the chintz, and two pieces were sewed together at the edge to make the inside and outside of the basket. All were then sewed together and tiny bows of scarlet ribbon put at the top of each seam. It was inexpensive, easily made, and very pretty, each design being distinct upon the soft groundwork.

But few articles that have the wrong side exposed are pretty for transfer work. is it is scarcely possible to make the reverse side neat. Collars, caps, and any lined articles are more effective than handkerchiefs or curtains on this account.

The last style of transfer work borders some what on the applique, and yet varies from that in the design, being always laid over the material, while in applique the upper material is as often the design stamped out.

To do this work when the design is prepared and the section attached, is simply a matter of care and patience; but if ladies wish to work profitably for fancy fairs or gift-making at a moderate price, they will do well to prepare their own work, and in no work can they make more saving than in transfer work. A bold design in illumination, the beautiful patterns constantly published in leading periodicals, and other patterns procurable at fancy stores, offer numerous designs for private use.

Having selected a design it is easy to procure scraps of colored cloth from a tailor's, and to cut out the forms to be placed upon the surface of the material for the article to be made.

Dark or light drab, the shades of mode, gray, stone-color, invisible green and brown will any of them wearfbetter than black or blue, and are quite as effective. But if the article contemplated is for a room, it is best to select the color best suited to the other furniture.

Carefully mark the middle of the cloth, and make other marks at regular distances, two, three, or four inches apart, according to the form of the design. Then attach the pieces of cloth cut with strong paste (starch is the cleanest kind of paste). Cover with a clean linen cloth, and press with a moderately hot iron until perfectly dry. It must be pressed over a soft surface, face downward.

Work round the design in buttonhole or satin stitch with split Berlin wool, the exact color of the groundwork, thus throwing the pattern into strong relief. A wool just one shade darker than the groundwork gives the pattern a raised appearance that is very rich, but if this is attempted great care must be taken to have every stitch perfectly even, or the work will have a jagged appearance that will ruin the effect.

A very handsome piano cover, in this work, was made of soft drab lady's cloth, with a border of large ivy leaves in dark green, sewed down with split Berlin wool one shade darker than the drab groundwork. In each corner were three ivy leaves in a graceful group. In the centre was a wreath of the ivy leaves, and the whole was finished by an embroidered monogram in green Berlin wool in the centre of the wreath. It was very handsome and every leaf was cut by the worker from the cloth, from an exact pattern made from an actual leaf. Each leaf was veined by long stitches in Berlin wool, one shade darker than the green cloth. Another piece of work by the same hand, may be here described; but will be almost too heavy and clumsy to tempt many imitators. It was made of a gentleman's shawl, such as was worn years ago, and which had been long lying useless. It was a mixed gray, and was very heavy. Upon this ground was put a border of flowers cut from the centre of a drugget, the border of which was entirely faded and worn out. These flowers were arranged at regular intervals, grouped at the corners, and firmly pasted and pressed down. The edges were then worked over in coarse gray yarn, and the edge of the shawl bound with Turkey red carpet binding. From two useless articles a very handsome floor cloth was thus obtained to replace the wornout drugget, and the worker was constantly asked by visitors where she had purchased that beautiful drugget.

Very pretty white aprons are made of Swiss muslin with embroidery cut from India muslin or wornout pieces of embroidered work, transferred neatly in the corners or on the border, and if neatly and strongly sewed they will wash as well and wear as long as if the embroidery was originally done on the muslin. It is also a beautiful finish for the Normandy caps of lace or muslin so much in fashion for little girls.

Indeed, many of the costly imported ones, made of real lace, have the embroidery that finishes them transferred, and they are much easier to do up, as the embroidery can be ripped off and sewed on again when the lace is washed, in a straight piece, whereas the embroidery upon the lace holds it in folds or puckers, often difficult to iron smoothly after the cap is wet.

We have seen a very pretty cap in this style, where the transferred sprigs upon the lace were also used for the ends of the ribbon, trimming it with good effect. Medallions of lace with sprigs of embroidery transferred in the centre, make a beautiful finish for neckties, scarfs and bows of ribbon, and are very popular.

But there is no branch of needlework where great neatness is more essential than in transferring, since any slovenly work will be so immediately apparent, both in the want of beauty in the article made and in its wear.

Fig. 85.—HANDKERCHIEF CORNER.

Handkerchief Corner in Transfer Work.

The work is in satin and spot stitch, carefully cut out and sewed down to a handkerchief corner, or upon the end of a necktie.

Tobacco-Bag in Japanese Transfer Work.

The material is glove kid, and the pattern in the Japanese work already described in this chapter. Line with oil-silk, and bind with kid of a color to match the pattern.

Fig. 86.

Border in Transfer Work.

In cloth, with the pattern in a differen color, worked on the edge in buttonhole stitch in two shades of crochet silk. The spots are embroidered in the same silk.

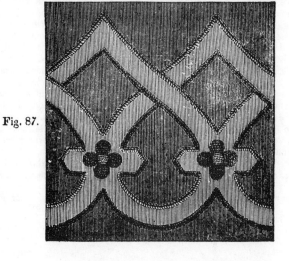

Fig. 87.

CHAPTER XII.

PERFORATED CARD WORK.

Never in the history of fancy work has there been a fashion more marked and popular than the present rage for every description of work upon perforated card. The varieties of articles are constantly increasing, and for the time, at least, this material and work has largely superseded all others.

The material is stiff card, pierced with minute holes at regular intervals, some of it being fine enough to require the finest cambric needle for working, while others are coarse enough to require double Berlin wool or chenille to fill the space. It can be obtained in large sheets or in cards cut for any purpose required, with ornamented borders.

It is made in many colors, and in gold-faced and silver-faced sheets.

The stitch for working is usually the cross-stitch of canvas work, but straight or diagonal lines are often used to fill up spaces where the cross-stitch would narrow or widen the pattern too much.

It is useful, for a great variety of fancy articles can be made to look as handsome as canvas work, and has the advantage of keeping in place without a frame, being stiff enough to hold easily, and not in danger of stretching.

In working, care must be taken that the needle, when threaded, does not stretch the hole in the card. Many wool needles that will slip very easily through unthreaded, will stretch the hole perceptibly when carrying the silk or wool required. Always test this before beginning any piece of work.

The small-sized patterns may be worked in silk or in split Berlin wool, both of which come in shaded as well as solid colors for this special work.

The coarser patterns can be worked in single or double Berlin wool or chenille.

Both fine and coarse card can be worked in beads, as these come in many sizes. They should exactly fit the spaces between the holes, but if this can not be done, it is better to have them a little too small than too large. Gold, silver, steel and colored beads all look well. Crystal beads worked in very bright colored silk, with a grounding of silk one shade lighter, are very effective. All bead work upon perforated card is greatly improved if the remainder of the card is covered by grounding, as in canvas work; but when silk or wool are used, the grounding can be used or not, as desired.

For any purpose where canvas work requires to be strained over a flat, stiff surface, perforated cardboard can be worked in perfect imitation, but must always be grounded. Any of the Berlin wool patterns can be worked in perforated card, but the fancy stores are now amply supplied with card already marked for every use to which it can be put.

Illuminated texts to bind and hang against the wall come already stamped in every size. Lettering for these is usually worked in shaded silk or wool, but the texts are varied with pictures, flowers and other designs requiring some skill and taste to embroider in the appropriate colors. The "Old Oaken Bucket," embroidered, as the writer has actually seen it, with a bright blue well and a purple bucket, was not effective, although the surrounding grass was very green, and the rope a fine shade of brown.

Book-markers are worked usually in silk or beads, and are sewn upon ribbons a little wider than the card, and more than double the length. All embroidery upon perforated card consists of a pattern worked upon a plain surface. It is of such combinations of color as will form wreaths, sprays and flowers, as well as lettering and set patterns, and any Berlin pattern will do for a model, stitch for stitch being taken.

When a great number of colors are used, and but little of each one, it is advisable to wind each shade and color upon a separate piece of card, that is notched to keep it from unwinding. Or a long piece of narrow card may be taken for one color, the shades being wound in order, one after another, along the length, and the card notched between.

Shaded wools are very effective, but when used care must be taken to match each fresh needleful exactly to the last stitch, or the work will look confused. If grounded, do not have the colors inharmonious. Shaded greens will look well upon a dark maroon ground, but not well upon a black ground, as the darker shades of the green are then lost.

Designs worked upon perforated card can often be advantageously grounded when the card has become soiled. In such a case, it is best to use a dull neutral color, or the embroidery may appear faded. Very often the colors in the embroidery will be quite fresh when the card is soiled and the trimming faded. If the card is then grounded in grey or brown, and fresh trimming added, an old, shabby article will appear quite fresh and bright.

Scratch My Back.

This is a simple little gift that a child may make of perforated card. A pretty wreath or border is first embroidered, and the words, "Scratch My Back," worked in the centre. It is then lined with bright colored silk, neatly bound, and has a ribbon loop to hang by. On the back is pasted neatly a large square piece of sandpaper, for scratching matches; or, the whole back may be made of sandpaper, bound in with the front with ribbon.

Fly-Traps.

These are made of perforated cards, small squares being cut, each one embroidered and bound, and six sewed together to form a block. Eight or ten are then fastened upon wires in some pretty form, each dangling loosely from the wire by a loop of ribbon. The wire must be covered with chenille. The whole is then suspended from a chandelier in the centre of the room, by a long ribbon, and its constant motion will drive away the flies from persons sitting near.

Card-Baskets.

The pieces for these can be obtained at any fancy store, with ornamented edges. They are to be embroidered, lined either with another piece of embroidered card or with silk, and tied together with bows of bright colored ribbon.

Lamp-Mats or Cologne-Stands.

These are embroidered in floss silk, upon finely perforated cards, in a handsome Berlin pattern. They are lined with silk, bound with ribbon, and then trimmed with quilled satin ribbon on the edges. Very handsome ones can be purchased with the pattern already stamped.

Needle-Books.

These are made of two squares of perforated card, embroidered in silk or wool in a Berlin pattern, lined with silk, and bound with ribbon. Pieces of flannel a little smaller are worked in buttonhole-stitch scallops with silk or split wool, and neatly bound together at one side with ribbon. The cards are then sewed together, with the flannel between, at one side, and ribbons sewed at the other side to tie them together. Very pretty needle-books, with but little work, are made by pasting French glaced pictures of birds or flowers upon the pieces of card, instead of embroidering them.

Illuminated Texts.

These may be purchased already stamped, or may be worked in German lettering from the Berlin letter patterns. When worked they should be lined with silk, bound with ribbon, and have a long ribbon, by which to be suspended to the wall, attached to each end at the top. Some of them are very elaborate and handsome, and they are generally worked in shaded wool or silk.

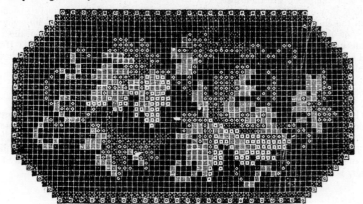

Fig. 88.

Cigar Case,

embroidered upon perforated card, in beads. A monogram or initial should be worked upon the other side. Both lined with silk, and bound with ribbon. To be sewed together at the sides and bottom, the top left open.

Shoe Bags.

These are made in perforated card of very coarse perforation, worked in double Berlin wool in a large pattern. The card is cut in a long slope at the sides, like a letter V. These are worked and lined with glazed cambric, and then bound with ribbon. When bound they are sewed together at the sloped edges to make a long cornucopia-shaped bag. The edges are trimmed with quilled ribbon. Four of these bags are then sewed together at the points and about half way up, and hang on the closet door to hold slippers.

These are very handsome mounted in walnut wood, to stand beside a bureau, or in a wardrobe.

Fig. 89.

Cologne Stand.

Worked in. Berlin wool and chenille upon perforated card-board, and trimmed with satin ribbon, put on the edge in box-pleats.

Book Mark.

Worked on perforated board, with floss silk, shaded, and sewed upon ribbon **three** times its length, looped at one end.

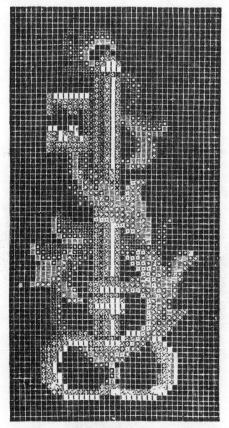

Fig. 90.

Needle Case of Perforated Card.

The cover of this needle-case consists of slanted squares of perforated card, fastened with ribbon bows, and measuring five inches in length and three and one-half in width.

This is of silver-faced perforated card, worked in long lines of colored silk, fastened with one white bead at each crossing, and with three white beads in each diamond.

It is trimmed with ribbon to match the silk, drawn down in puffs with a string of five white beads on each side.

Two or three leaves of fine flannel, cut out in scallops around the edge, are fastened in.

Fig. 91.

CHAPTER XIII.

PERSIAN RUG WORK.

This work, coming properly under the head of knitting, is of sufficient importance, at the present date, to merit a chapter by itself. It is the latest caprice of fashion, in fancy work, and while requiring taste, and a great deal of patience, is of such beauty as to amply repay the time and labor expended upon it. The rugs, when completed, are a perfect imitation of Persian carpet, are thick, soft, and beautiful, and at the same time very durable.

They are made of the ravelled worsted of tapestry Brussels carpet, which is crimped by weaving into wavy threads, that are a most delightful mat under the foot. These are knit together with a very firm, strong back of crochet cotton.

The first process is to ravel the worsted, and while a child, properly taught, can do this perfectly well, carelessly done by any fingers, it will have a straggling, uneven end, that will not look well when finished.

Some knit with very long pieces of worsted, some with very short ones; some on large needles, some on fine. If the worsted is too long, it falls over and mats under the foot; if too short, it shows the cotton back. If the needles are too large, the rug is straggling and uneven; if too fine, the colors are crowded.

The great beauty lies in a soft surface, long enough to half bury the foot, firm and even. To secure this, the directions below are given. Longer or shorter threads depend upon the width of the strips of carpet cut.

Remnants of new tapestry Brussels can be purchased in any carpet or upholsterer's store.

The carpet will be found to have a back of evenly-woven linen threads. Cut between these threads in a perfectly straight line, from selvedge to selvedge, the best length being when fifteen threads are between the cuts. When the carpet is in long strips, so cut, trim off the selvedge and carefully ravel out the long linen threads upon each side. And here the care is required to keep the worsted ends firm, as they will soon split if the long thread is drawn down in quick jerks. Take the long threads from each side till only three are left in the middle.

Now remove the short linen threads, and the worsted will draw out in short crimped lengths of every shade and color. Cut the remaining long threads often, to keep the worsted firm and even. When the worsted is ravelled it should be kept in a wide, shallow pasteboard box, without any pressure, as the beauty of the rug depends very much upon these threads being kept light and springy. It

Is well to divide them into boxes of dark and light color, without other regard to color, unless a border is knit, when it is well to keep the color intended for that in a separate box.

No. 8 crochet cotton, and No. 12 steel knitting-needles, make a firm back.

Set up thirty stitches of cotton, and knit three rows of the cotton alone. Then knit in this manner :

4th row.—Slip one stitch, knit one, put one of the worsted threads over the right-hand needle, being very careful to have it doubled over the needle exactly in the middle, with the two ends the same length : knit the third stitch, put on another thread of worsted, repeat until the last two stitches ; knit these plain.

5th row.—Slip one, knit one, take up the worsted and third stitch together, and knit as one stitch ; knit in this way, taking up the worsted and cotton together in every stitch to the end of the row.

6th row.—Same as 4th.

7th row.—Same as 5th.

Alternate in this way till your strip is about four feet long, when knit three plain rows of the cotton and cast off.

No regularity need be observed in taking up the threads of worsted excepting to mix light and dark colors together well, as the more variegated the colors the better the effect.

Three strips make a good sized rug, when the border is added.

Fifteen stitches are sufficient for the border, and when knit it must be left sufficiently long to allow for the ends.

When all the strips are done, crochet them together on the back with chain stitch, in the same cotton used for the knitting.

An expert knitter can knit the border in with the middle, but it requires more attention to keep the colors separate.

There are a great variety of ways of bordering the Persian rugs, and all are handsome. One we have seen is of variegated colors in the centre, the dark and light well mingled, and has a border of vivid scarlet predominating, though the carpet threads are never a solid color, being tipped or mixed always with other colors than the leading one.

A second one has the centre of dark worsted, the border of light.

A third has a light centre, and border of rich green predominating.

When the knitting is done, the strips fastened together, the whole must be lined with strong heavy canvas to keep it in place. No handsomer rug for drawing-room, hall, or library has ever been made, and it can suit any carpet or furniture by having a border to match the predominating color of its surroundings.

CHAPTER XIV.

PATCHWORK.

Although this work seems to come more under the head of plain than fancy needlework, this little book would scarcely be complete were all reference to it omitted. It is generally our first work and our last—the schoolgirl's little fingers setting their first crowded or straggling stitches of appalling length in patchwork squares, while the old woman, who can no longer conquer the intricacies of fine work, will still make patchwork quilts for coming generations.

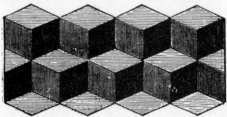

Fig. 92.

But the calico squares whose combinations and varieties would fill a volume are not the only patchwork that is made. Silk is also used in variously shaped blocks and patterns, for the covers of chairs and bed-quilts, although we have known many pieces, started in tiny pieces to make an enormous bed-quilt, end ignominiously in a very small pincushion.

The taste is one that has nearly died out, although some beautiful specimens are still seen at fancy fairs, the work of tasteful brains and industrious fingers.

Where any scope is given to fancy in patchwork, the pieces should be basted over stiff card, or, still better, pieces of tin, and sewed over and over, the card being then removed. Some run the pieces together, some sew them on the sewing-machine, but the old-fashioned overstitch will ever be the best for patchwork. It is a great improvement upon the huge and unwieldy quilting-frames of the days of our grandmothers, to make the patchwork for a quilt in bound squares. Each one is lined, first with wadding, then with calico quilted neatly, and bound with strips of calico. These squares being then sewed together, the quilt is complete. Album quilts made in this way, with the name of the giver neatly written upon a small square of white in the centre of each piece, are much more acceptable than when they must all be quilted together in a huge frame.

CHAPTER XV.

TAMBOUR WORK

Although somewhat out of date, this style of fancy work is beautiful enough to be revived, and the taste and ingenuity of the present day applied to making new combinations in the stitch.

The design for the work is stamped or drawn on the material, which is then stretched evenly in an embroidery frame.

The tambour needle is hooked at the end precisely like a crochet needle, and is of steel screwed firmly into an ivory handle. The stitch is a single chain stitch in crochet, taken through the material in colored silk.

The needle is held under the work, and pushed through and drawn back for each stitch.

Follow the outline of the pattern carefully in fine crochet chain stitches drawn through, and afterwards fill up the pattern thus outlined with close lines of the same stitch, in the same color.

This work may be done on any material from heavy cloth to finest net, but is so little in use, that no more space will be devoted to it in this book.

9

CHAPTER XVI.

WIRE WORK.

Wire work is, strictly speaking, simply a foundation for other materials, and is in use as a framework for many pretty fancy articles where it is entirely concealed. It should be selected at once strong and pliable, and always covered either with thread closely twisted over it, or with ribbon wound round very closely and firmly.

When thus prepared it can be used as a foundation for bead work, chenille work, hanging baskets of any material, vases, stands, indeed, any articles requiring a stiff skeleton frame. It makes a very pretty cover for window flower pots, when twisted into the proper shape after being covered with double Berlin wool crochet work in a double stitch.

Before covering wire for any fancy work, every spot of rust should be carefully rubbed off with fine emery paper.

Wire and Bead Basket for Worsted.

To make this basket double a piece of covered wire eighteen inches and a half long so as to form a ring nine inches and a quarter in circumference. In a similar manner form a ring ten inches in circumference of a piece of wire twenty inches long, and cover both rings closely with blue floss silk. Then take two pieces of wire each seventy-six inches long, lay them on each other in such a manner that one end of each piece of wire projects from the end of the other piece half an inch, wind blue silk on both pieces at the same time, and bend the double wire thus formed into ten loops, each three inches and three-quarters long, which meet as shown in the illustration. Fasten the projecting ends of the wire together. Wind crystal beads that have been strung on blue silk closely on every piece of wire, fasten the wire loops together with blue silk, and overhand them on both rings with blue silk. The smaller ring forms the bottom and the larger ring the upper edge of the basket. For the bottom cut, besides, a circular piece of cardboard two inches and three-quarters in diameter, and cover it on both sides with blue silk; on that side which afterward comes on the inside of the basket cover the cardboard with a piece of wire covered with silk and beads, which is sewed on in coils. For the lining of the basket cut a straight strip of blue silk twenty inches long and four inches and three-quarters wide; hem the sides and join the ends; then gather the silk on one side, and overhand it together with the outer edge of the bottom. Fasten the bottom and lining inside of the basket, sewing the former to the lower bead ring with double blue silk. Sew the upper edge of the lining, which is also gathered, to the upper bead ring. The handle, which is formed of double wire fourteen inches long and covered with beads, is set on as shown by the illustration.

Fig. 93.—WIRE AND BEAD BASKET FOR WORSTED.

CHATER XVII.

DOLL-DRESSING.

Most girls wno uke work at all are very fond of dressing dolls; not so much, perhaps, at the age when they play with them themselves, but when they grow older, and they dress them for their younger sisters, or, if they have none, for little girls of their acquaintance. A doll is a nice present for a child at any time, but how much the pleasure is enhanced if it is dressed! Not dressed as they dress them in some shops, with only a few clothes, and made so that they will not take off and on; but with every article of clothing, as if it were a real child; and, above all things, a nightgown! Some children are quite content with putting their dolls to bed in their clothes, or, what is even worse undressing them and leaving them so, having no nightgown to put them in!

We will begin with the

Nightgown.

Get some fine calico to commence with; always use fine stuff of every sort, for the dolls being so small, the clothes set very badly if made of thick material.

Cut out the front and back, as at Nos. 1 and 2; then the shoulder-piece, No. 3; then run the front and back together under the arm, gathering the back into the shoulder-pieces; then join them over the shoulder; then putting on them a small narrow band, slightly gathering the fronts into it, putting the pieces at the back in plain, and then the sleeves,

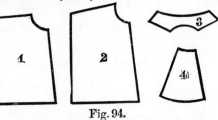

Fig. 94.

No. 4. The trimming is, of course, according to fancy—some insertion up the front, with very narrow goffered frills up each side, looks very nice; also tatting or crochet; indeed, anything of the sort; but it certainly looks better trimmed. A great improvement to the nightgown is to cut the fronts too broad across for the doll, and run narrow tucks down to the waist; but this is, of course, more difficult, as the tucks want to be run very evenly.

Chemise.

A doll's chemise is a very easy thing to make. Cut out in calico two pieces in the shape of Fig. 95 ; run them neatly together, and down the sides and over the shoulders ; then cut the front open a little way down. Hem the neck and sleeves all round with a very narrow hem, and make a broad one round the bottom of the chemise. If trimming is required, a little lace round the neck and sleeves makes a pretty finish.

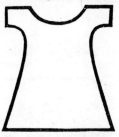
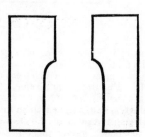

Fig. 95.—CHEMISE. Fig. 96.—DRAWERS.

Drawers.

Next the drawers. Cut out two legs similar to the pattern given ; run them up ; then join the legs together just at the top in front, only running it a very short way down. Then make a very narrow hem round each leg, and a nice broad one at the bottom ; gather it into a band, putting a button or strings to it. A little lace edging round the legs, or two or three narrow tucks, look very nice.

Bodice for the Petticoat.

A flannel petticoat is, of course, a very easy thing to make. A piece of white or red fine flannel, herringboned round the bottom, and gathered into a band at the waist, with buttons or strings. For most of the underclothes I should recommend very small linen buttons ; strings are so untidy. The white or upper petticoat should be made of white calico or twill, rather full, with a broad hem at the bottom, and I should recommend a good deep tuck ; it makes the frock stand out so well. The body can be made in two ways : either off the skirt or on ; but I

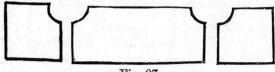

Fig. 97.

think that it is decidedly the best to sew it on. Cut it in three pieces, as in Fig. 97, join them together under the arm, make a hem at the top of each of the pieces and the bottom ; then sew the skirt (which must be gathered) on to it, and run draw-strings in it.

Now that we have finished the under-linen, we must begin about the dresses. Never make them of a *thick* stuff, and always be sure to choose a small pattern, or, better still, no pattern at all. Unless the doll is very large, it is always best to make a low body, as it is so difficult to make the neck set well.

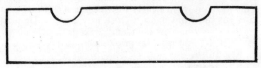

Fig. 98.

Bodice for Dress.

The skirt is, of course, as easy as possible to make; simply to run the seams and make a broad hem. A low-necked bodice should be made in this way: A long, narrow piece, with a place cut out for the sleeves (see Fig. 98); hem up the backs. Then cut out the sleeves, as in No. 2; run the seams of the sleeves, and then sew them into the arm-holes, placing the seam of the sleeve even with that of the body; gather the other end of the sleeve into a little narrow band; gather the body at the top and the bottom into narrow bands. Some white lace in the sleeves and neck finishes it off very nicely, and a sash always looks pretty.

The best way of making a high body is to cut it out similar to the patterns I give in Nos. 3 and 4; stitch them together under and over the arm; cut out the sleeves, as at No. 5, and sew them in the arm-hole, keeping the seam well round to the back. Then put a very narrow band on the neck; hem up the backs and put some tiny hooks on, and make the loops.

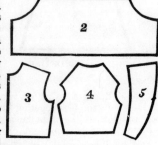

Fig. 99.

Pinafore.

The prettiest kind of pinafore is, I think, at No. 1. This must be cut in four pieces—the front, No. 2; the backs, as at No. 3; and the apron, No. 4. Then join the front and backs over the arms, also the apron and bib; then hem the backs and all round the apron and the arm-holes and neck, making these hems narrower. Stitch a piece of tape along the front and along both of the backs, through which run the string, and also run one round the neck. A lace edging all round the apron and round the arm-holes looks very nice. This sort of pinafore is best made in diaper or Holland; if the latter, substitute white braid for lace edging.

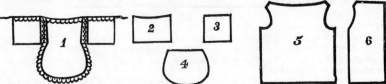

Fig. 100.—PINAFORE.   FIG. 101.—ANOTHER.

Another Pinafore.

Another sort of pinafore is to cut out a plain long front, as at No. 5, and back as at No. 6; join them under and over the arm, and hem it all round, running a string round the neck. It may be left plain or gathered in at the front, putting a small ornamental piece on in front, trimmed with narrow lace.

Jackets.

Jackets are almost the hardest thing to make for dolls—especially if they are made of velvet or a thick cloth. The best material to make then of is, of course,

Fig. 102.

black silk. Cut the fronts out, as at No. 1, and the back as in No. 2; the sleeves, No. 3. Then it is better to bind it all round with braid, which sets better and is less clumsy than a hem.

Dresses for China Dolls.

The best way to make little china dolls' dresses is all in one; a long straight piece joined at the back, and hemmed round the bottom; two holes cut for the arms, and then turned down at the neck and gathered, drawing it up not tight round the neck, but just on to the shoulder, so that you can fasten it off, and yet leave room to pass it over the head; tie a sash round the waist, and the doll is dressed. A petticoat made in the same way is all that is required; anything else does not set—the dolls being so small, it makes them look simply like a bundle of clothes. A cloak is the best thing f r these sort of dolls for an out-door garment. Cut this in the shape of a half-moon, and in the middle of the straight side cut out a small piece for the neck. Make this in red llama, or some soft thin material, and bind it round with narrow black ribbon without an edge. Hats can be made on a shape made with cap wire, and then trimmed; but a very good plan is to get the lid of a pill-box—of course it must fit the doll's head—and cover it with black velvet, and it makes a charming little turban hat.

I have not as yet said a word about boy dolls. There is but one way in which they can be made to look nice—I mean big dolls.

Boys' Knickerbockers.

A dark blue serge, black velvet, or, if in summer, holland, are the best stuffs to make them of. I give a pattern of the knickerbockers at No. 1, Fig. 103. Each leg must be run up and then joined together, making a hem round the bottom, in which run some elastic; and it is a very good way to sew them on to a broad elastic band, which will, of course, stretch, so that the knickerbockers can be taken off and on.

Tunic.

A tunic is the best thing to make for boy dolls, and it is best to cut it in two pieces, as in No. 2, Fig. 103; join the sides together, and hem it round the bottom. Put in the sleeves, and cut an opening down the front, so that it may be put over the doll's head. It is best to bind it with narrow braid round the neck and down the front, which must be buttoned with tiny buttons, and then a band round the waist.

The men in the dolls' house are very hard to dress, and it is, I think, almost impossible to make their things to come off and on. The shirt must, of course, be thought of first; but there is no necessity to make a whole shirt—merely a

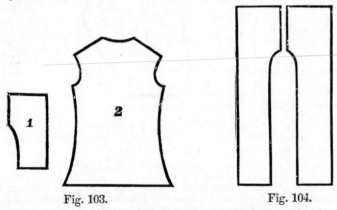

Fig. 103.   Fig. 104.

front with two pieces to pass over the back. A small collar must be attached to this, under which must be passed a narrow piece of ribbon to form a tie. The trousers must be cut in two pieces (Fig. 104), and joined together. The waistcoat is simply two pieces crossed over from the back, with two or three buttons, which are easily made with bits of black silk, sewed up into little rounds to imitate them. The coat is made in the same way exactly as the one I described for the big doll—of course, altered as to size. It does not do to make either the shirt or the waistcoat entirely, as it makes the coat set so badly.

Costume Dolls.

NORMANDY PEASANT.

The underclothing for this costume should be full, and reaching just below the knees; the dress petticoat of red merino or delaine, trimmed with three rows of narrow black velvet at equal distances, and just a little longer than the under petticoat; black velvet bodice with long points behind and before, cut square and laced up the front; white muslin sleeves coming just below the elbow, left loose and rather full; white muslin half-handkerchief crossed upon the chest and over the bodice; muslin apron with pockets; gold beads round the neck, and gold cross; long gold ear-rings; a rosary hung from the left side; thick shoes and white stockings, or, if it is a china doll, the feet can be painted to imitate them.

If you are dressing a small china doll, take for the cap a piece of stiff white writing-paper, about one and one-half to one and three-quarter inches in depth; for the length measure round the doll's head, allowing a little piece on each side to admit of the paper being bent up the back, as in Fig. 105. Cover the paper with muslin, and trim round the forehead and up the ends with very narrow lace; sew up the cap at the bend in the paper; fill up the top to form the crown with muslin gathered in; press out the flaps behind until they present this appearance (Fig 106)—

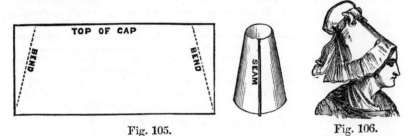

Fig. 105.   Fig. 106.

This completes the costume. If the doll is larger, of course the height of the cap must be increased, as it is the chief characteristic of the dress.

ITALIAN PEASANT.

The underclothing is the same as for the Normandy peasant, except being a little longer. Dress skirt of blue or any bright-colored merino, trimmed with three or four rows of different-colored braids, either vandyked or straight round the skirt; bodice of black velvet, with small basque behind, cut low in the neck; and open stomacher laced across, with braids to match the skirt; the neck of the bodice to be trimmed with a muslin tucker; white muslin sleeves to the wrist, either open or closed; black velvet ribbon round the neck, with a cross hanging on the chest; a rosary hung from the left side; thin black shoes and white stockings.

If the doll is the same size as the Normandy peasant, take for the cap a piece of white writing-paper, about two inches in length and one and one-half inches in width; place it on the doll's head lengthways; then bend the paper so as to make it fall close to the back of the head. Cover the paper with muslin, and trim round with lace. The cap may be kept in shape by drawing your thread tight from the crown to the top of the flap behind—of course, from underneath.

The costume is now complete. If you are dressing china dolls, the best thing to fasten the caps on to the head is liquid glue.

SPANISH DANCER.

The underskirts are very short, and several of them made of tarlatan, pinked out; muslin drawers, wide and very full. The dress may be made of any bright-colored silk or satin, trimmed with black lace flounces, and short. The bodice should be a low square, and sleeves to the elbow, trimmed with lace to match the skirt. On the hands there should be long mittens, and in the hair a high comb and red rose, with black lace mantilla thrown over the comb, and fastened on the side with the rose. Either boots or shoes may be worn, bronze or gold-color.

MARQUISE DRESS.

To show off this dress the doll should be of good size. Make the underclothing —consisting of chemise, flannel petticoat, white petticoats—all very nice, and very much trimmed. For the dress petticoat have a piece of white or rose-colored satin, trimmed across the front with lace. For the train, a handsome piece of brocaded satin, trimmed up the sides and round the train with lace. The bodice is cut square behind, and sleeves to the elbow, trimmed with lace. There should be a stomacher made of the same material as the skirt petticoat, all made of the same brocade as the train. Shoes, with high heels, rosettes, and silk stockings.

To make the doll complete she should have long straight hair, which must be rolled back from the forehead on a cushion, and the hair from the back of head must be rolled up on another cushion, with a long curl hanging from the left side, with a flat bow in the hair to match the skirt. The hair must be powdered, and on the face two or three black patches ; one on the forehead towards the left side, one on the chin to the right, and one on each cheek. This completes the dress.

CHAPTER XVIII.

MISCELLANEOUS.

Card Basket in Panama Canvas.

This pretty trifle is a combination of Panama canvas and straw work, finished with wheat heads. The straws are placed in three bars fastened at the top by a ribbon and widening at the bottom like the frame for a gipsy camp-kettle. At the top is a cluster of wheat heads. About an inch from the bottom is sewed to the straw sticks a piece of stiff card cut in a triangular shape.

Over this is laid a square of Panama canvas fringed upon each edge and embroidered in the centre and corners in a small Berlin pattern. It is secured with tiny stitches here and there to the card, but must appear to lie loosely there.

Picture Frames in Crochet.

These frames are made of curtain rings. Over each one is a line of crochet work in Berlin wool of perfect wood color. When a sufficient number are worked, a frame must be made of wood covered with moss-green velvet. Upon this the rings are sewn, the wood being the exact width of one ring. But two are sewn, one on each edge, meeting in the middle in a slope and fastened so together. In the corners four meet in the same way.

The effect is very pretty, and the colors may be changed by covering the frame with brown velvet and the rings with green chenille or Berlin wool.

Travelling Case.

The material is fine French kid, lined throughout with oil silk of the best quality. The embroidery, which can be simple or elaborate, according to the worker's time or fancy, is in fine worsted braid.

The case is about eleven inches in length. Cut the ends and sides according to the design Fig. 107, and bind round with ribbon; a strap of the same is placed across the centre. Two short straps are sewn on the inside lining to hold the nail and tooth brush. This case can either be folded up or hung on the wall.

Fig. 108 shows it folded and tied for travelling. In ocean travelling it can hang upon the stateroom door, and if fastened with loops at all, the corners will keep its contents undisturbed by any motion of the steamer.

Fig. 107.—TRAVELLING CASE—OPEN.

Fig. 108.—TRAVELLING CASE—CLOSED.

Fig. 109.—RUG PATTERN FOR A TRAVELLING BAG.

Rug Pattern for a Travelling Bag.

To bring before our readers large rug patterns in the pages of our small volume would be impossible; in order therefore to give them an oversight of a very uncommon pattern for travelling bag, we have chosen this, seen only in a small size, which, however, to our readers will be a sufficient guide on account of the clear plate and little complication of color.   The desired size of the bag is made from the coarseness of the canvas; our model, worked in Berlin wool, is thirteen inches deep and sixteen and a quarter inches wide; black being the darkest shade, three others follow in gray and milk white for the lighter colors; in this shading the upper part of the railway truck is worked, the luggage and the shades between the wheels; the latter itself is for the most part black, steel, a little light gray and white; the axletrees and so-called "puffer" on the railway carriage are of steel and gold beads, the latter being of the lightest color; the letters and edge marked out light, are on the front side of the carriage to be of gold beads.   The pointed scroll frame bordered with yellow silk enclosing the scarlet ground of the centre part, is filled up with white silk, and matches the light points in the large scroll shapes of a blue green shading in four colors, with a light silk edge; for the plain edge, on the contrary, between the black ground, pea green in one color and again in silk, is to be chosen; for the ground part dark blue gives a nice effect.

Hairpin Baskets.

These very pretty additions to the toilet table or dressing bureau are easily made, ornamental and convenient.   The baskets can be purchased at any fancy store, if desired, filled with horse hair and covered with a very coarse white net tacked over neatly on the top.   The top is then knit in the following manner :

Set up thirty stitches on steel needles, rather coarse; knit one line across, the second line, place the thread for every stitch over the forefinger of the left hand to form a loop, and knit this loop as a stitch, knit the third row plain, the fourth like the second, and so alternate the rows till you have a perfect square.   Put this over the basket top and sew the edges down firmly, letting the loops stand up.

If the basket is round, crochet a circle for the top, as described for the knitting.

If a basket is inconvenient to procure, cut four pieces of perforated card exactly alike, about four inches long and three wide, and a fifth piece three inches each way.   Upon the four pieces embroider some pretty Berlin wool pattern—a monogram or initial is pretty upon one piece.

Bind all five pieces with bright colored ribbon, but they need not be lined. Sew the edges of the four pieces together, lengthwise, to form a square, and sew the fifth piece on for the bottom.   Fill with coarse horse hair, and cover with lace and the knitted top already described.   Finish at the corners with little bows of the same ribbon as the binding, or tassels of the Berlin wool.

A pincushion to match, covered with embroidered canvas, and filled with sawdust, makes an extremely pretty set for a toilet table.

A pair made upon silver-faced perforated card, embroidered in moss roses and leaves, bound with pale blue, covered with pale blue knitting, and finished with blue satin ribbon, quilled on the edges, will make a pretty Christmas gift.

Scrap Bags.

These are pretty combinations of perforated card and crochet work, very useful and popular.   Cut a piece of card, coarsely perforated, about four inches wide and eighteen inches long.   Work it in an arabesque pattern, key border, or border of leaves and flowers, in gay colored Berlin wools. Make an edge of buttonhole stitch, one stitch to each square perforated with double Berlin wool. Then sew the edges together at the ends to make a circle.

Crochet an edge at the top in shell pattern. At the bottom continue the shells, row after row, to make the bag, narrowing when near the end by knitting the shells in three stitches instead of four, then in two, then one, and omitting these last alternately till only one stitch is left on the crochet hook.

Make two heavy tassels of the Berlin wool for the end of the bag. Crochet a handle in double stitch from one side to the other of the top edge, to hang the bag by. Finish by covering the seam in the perforated card, with a large bow of ribbon, or crochet rosette, with a corresponding one on the other side. Vivid scarlet will wear better than any other color. The bag may be lined.

Tippets and Shoes.

To learn to find a use for everything, so that nothing is wasted, should form a part of a woman's education. Not only is it applicable in cooking, where such a knowledge is eminently useful, but in everything, a ready wit, an energetic mind, and busy fingers will find that "no fragment need be lost." Beautifully does Nature set us this example; all that seems waste and refuse she turns to account; and in like manner shall we find, if so disposed, what seems to us rubbish can be converted into use for others, if not for ourselves. For instance, the edges of new flannel, which are torn off, make excellent warm capes for poor little children, laid in rows one a little over the edge of the other, and run together, and bound with scarlet braid. The same material makes capital baby-shoes, run together in the same manner, lined with scarlet or blue flannel, and bound with the same colored ribbon. Balls can be also made with this list, which would be a great delight to children in an asylum; and few charitable actions are more appreciated than the giving toys to these little creatures, who have no possessions of their own, not even the clothes they wear, and whose faces light with wondrous pleasure at these small gifts. A pill-box must first be procured, and in it some shot or peas placed; then the list must be rolled over and over until it becomes round; over this must be wound some Berlin wool, of any color, closely over the list, so as to entirely conceal it; then, in a different color, which will harmonize with it, a chain-stitch must be worked all over it, like net-work.

Evening dresses, white or colored tarletan, old flannels, washed out muslins, or indeed any old material, torn in long narrow strips, and knitted upon large wooden needles in plain knitting stitch, form very warm and really pretty quilts, which would delight the heart of some poor old woman, and fully carry out the injunction to let "nothing be lost." The pieces must be very narrow. Join them together by lapping the ends over each other and running each edge with very strong cotton, and roll into balls before commencing to knit.

Ten or twelve stitches will be enough for each strip, and each should be about two yards long. Sew the strips together, as many as will make the required width.

For people with poor eyesight, or those who are desirous of improving the half light of long summer evenings, this is very nice work, rapidly done, and useful when completed, while requiring no skill or eyesight.

Colored Rugs and Mattresses.

These are two very useful presents to our poor neighbors, which would advantageously fill time. A piece of coarse packing-cloth must be procured, and cut to the size and width of an ordinary hearth rug, and on this must be sewn, in rows, pieces of colored cloth, which can be got at the tailors' from their old pattern-books—they will give them to their customers. Each row of cloth must be put over the other, to hide where they are sewn on. A common black worsted fringe sewn round the edge finishes the work nicely, and they wear for years. Mattresses stuffed with paper—that is, old newspapers and letters torn to pieces—and covered with a bright patchwork, are invaluable presents to poor mothers with young babies. Whilst they are washing and ironing or cooking, "baby" may be put down to crawl on the mattress, and the bright colors will so engage its attention that it will "coo" long stories to it, and try to scratch the colors up in its hands, and be so happy and busy that "mother" will bless the mattress and the kind young lady who made it. The tearing of the paper for the stuffing may be entrusted to the younger members of a family, who will greatly enjoy this variety in their employments, which might be given them to do in that hour between the light and the dark, when, weary of play, the little ones grow sleepy and, it must be owned, somewhat cross; the curious love of destruction which appears really a natural sin will be turned to good account in this manner, and the tearing up any amount of paper into tiny pieces will be enormous fun.

Frames for Photographs.

These are now made very prettily in card; silk, wool, or cotton being all used for the thread to cover them. Take two pieces of quite square card, according to the sized frame you require. Put them over each other, as shown in the en graving.

Fig. 110.

Take a skein of gold-colored floss silk and commence to wind from corner to corner, as in the engraving. Have three skeins of dark brown crochet silk, fine; take an end of each, and begin winding as before, until the cards are entirely covered, with the exception of the centre, which will be left for the portrait. Large white-headed pins must be put at each corner, to prevent the cotton slipping, which adds also to the prettiness of the frame.

Tapestry Rug.

This is a warm and excessively pretty rug to put down either before a dressing-table or under a library table, and would, I think, be a better present to some clergyman friend than the slippers, sermon-cases, and book-markers, which are showered often too liberally on the "new minister." I know one who was embarrassed with twenty pairs of slippers not made up!

The material required is fleecy wool—black, white, and a few bright colors. These are made into a fringe on a wooden mesh with a groove on one side; the wool is fastened to the mesh with coarse crochet cotton in a loop-stitch, and is cut off by running a pair of sharp scissors along the groove. This fringe is sewn on to a piece of coarse Hessian cut to the size you wish your rug to be. Black wool must be sewn all round, as a border, first, then the colors tastefully arranged in the centre, in imitation of carpet.

All sorts of short pieces joined in one make a very good fringe, and thus use up the bits left over from embroidery, knitting, or canvas work, and save the expense of new material.

Church Decorating.

Needlework is a way in which even quite young girls may materially help in the decoration of a church, though they should be careful not to attempt any delicate or difficult kinds, such as silk embroidery for altar cloths, or satin-work for chalice-veils and burses, without really learning of some professed worker to do it. But there are many easier pieces of work which almost any one with a little patience can do, such as markers for the books at the prayer-desk and on the altar. These may be embroidered in silk on ribbon. Or crosses or monograms may be cut out in cardboard, and either covered with gold or white beads, or made of a number of pieces of perforated cardboard, each one, one row of holes smaller than the last, so that the top one is the very narrowest strip possible. These, fastened together with gum, have the appearance of carving. Or, again, patterns may be cut in the cardboard so as to look almost as fine as lace. In each case, when finished, the crosses must be fastened on ribbon; it is best, if possible, to sew them on, as in a damp church gum or glue are so apt to give way. Kneeling-cushions in either cloth embroidery or worsted work, altar-carpets, pieces of velvet to hang from the pulpit-desk embroidered in gold silk, sermon-cases, etc., are other pieces of work quite easy to be done.

Case for Holding Point Lace, Embroidered on Panama Canvas.

Materials.—Light brown Panama canvas, 79 inches dark brown sarcenet ribbon, 3-4 inch wide, brown silk, light and dark brown, red, green, corn, blue and black purse silk, fine gold cord, 6 black buttons, etc.

This pretty and useful case, shown (Figs. 111 and 112) open and closed, requires for the foundation a straight piece of Panama canvas, thirteen and one-half inches long, and five and one-half inches wide; the middle of the canvas is then covered in the length with a row of cross-stitch in black purse silk; this is again covered with rows of the same, in a reversed order, of corn blue, green and red silk. The single stitches across, marking themselves in the pattern, are to be worked with gold. The border edging, the middle design of loose

10

stitches, in two shades of brown, shows the darkest shade as the outer edge. The inner arrangement of the case is of two pockets, two and three-quarter inches deep, of brown silk, taken double with a calico foundation, which are intended to hold the lace, tape, scissors, needles, etc., these pockets being put on the canvas ground lined with calico and silk, and joined to this by a brown silk binding,

Fig. 111.—OPEN.

stitched on twice. At the edge of one pocket, underneath the string of the case, of silk ribbon twelve and one-half inches long, to be sewn on at the outside and finished with bows, a piece of brown cord fastened at one of the ends, makes the holder for the different reels of thread. The loose end of this cord is then made with a loop, and buttoned to a button put on to correspond. A piece of wax

Fig. 112.—CLOSED.

cloth, four and one-quarter inches wide, bound all round with sarcenet ribbon, the length being as desired, and having a silk loop at each corner, is as a practical foundation for the point lace, fastened flat on the bottom of the case by a button sewn on without being creased in any way. The case is closed as seen when rolled up, by a button and brown silk loop.

Scrap Basket, for Work Table.

This basket is intended to catch bits of material, thread, or any odds and ends of sewing that make a work table or carpet untidy.

It is opened for use, and the top folded back protects the embroidery.

Materials—Sarcenet; ribbon to match, one inch broad; small pieces of black velvet; fine gold cord; gold thread; gold and chalk beads, etc.

Our model is made of yellow and black cane bars, about ten inches in diameter and eight and one-half inches high. The bottom has a plain silk lining; the rest has a full lining to set in puffs between the bars. The full-puffed lining is drawn together in the middle by a ribbon rosette. The ruche round the basket must

Fig. 113.

correspond with this. A plain lining is also required of cardboard and silk. Straps and pockets are placed inside.

A second lining of full muslin in the cover with a running and cord forms a closed bag. The embroidered drapes on the outside must be arranged according to the size of the basket. Both the appliques of black velvet must be fastened upon sarcenet of the same color as the lining, with gold cord. The remaining ornamentation is in gold and chalk beads, and long tufted stitches worked with gold cord and gold thread. The scallops are edged with gold cord, and ornamented with bows like the cover.

Wall Pockets.

To be really handsome these should be finished in walnut or satin wood at an upholsterer's, but if that is not practicable, may be made in the following way:

Embroider upon cloth or canvas a large and handsome pattern for the front, and one for the top of the back piece. When finished, stretch over a very thin board, cut in the desired shape, and fasten by long stitches across and across the back.

Cover a corresponding piece of pasteboard with the lining silk, and sew the edges of the embroidery and silk together, leaving the embroidered top of the back longer than the front piece.

About half way down the back piece begin to stitch a piece of silk about a quarter of a yard wide. Fasten this upon each side edge, both of the front and back pieces. At the bottom draw the silk together in small plaits till the front and back pieces meet, and sew them strongly together across the bottom, leaving the top to hang out loosely from the back.

A much more elegant pocket has the embroidery set into carved walnut or satin wood and joined by an upholsterer. These make very handsome presents for a gentleman's library, and answer that oft-repeated complaint:

" If it were for a lady, I could make a thousand things, but one never knows what to make to please a gentleman."

A handsome wall-pocket, with a monogram embroidered in the centre of a handsome wreath, will be sure to please any gentleman of taste.

Shoe Bags.

These are made of furniture chintz, bound with gay cotton braid, with compartments run for each pair of shoes or boots. They are very convenient where closet room is limited.

Scrap-Books and Screens.

The picture newspapers must be collected, and some nursery books pressed into the service, which the children will be proud to give, with the joy of being allowed to cut the pictures out. Anything will do—a head, a hand or foot, a portion of a dress, a bunch of flowers, trees, birds, butterflies—all carefully cut out—will work in beautifully. The screen is somewhat expensive to have made, but a second-hand one can be bought, and covered with white paper well strained over it. On this the pictures must be carefully stuck with strong well made paste, sufficiently close to cover all the paper; or if a colored paper—green, blue, or black—is preferred, the pictures might be grouped only on it, taking care to make some kind of connection between them; for instance, at an open attic window a bird might be placed as though it had just flown in, and the figure of a little girl placed near it would appear to be watching it. The figures out of the toy-books make capital subjects. One side of the screen plain and one colored form a pleasant variety; and when well done, it would be a great amusement in some invalid's room; they might lie, when weary of reading, finding out the different pictures, and weaving fanciful tales for them, which would while away the long hours, made so much longer by pain and suffering.

Scrap-books made in the same way are most acceptable presents either to little children before they can read, or still more to hospitals for sick children or the aged and bedridden. One containing sacred pictures and illuminated texts for

Sunday amusement would be very acceptable, and one full of bright-colored funny pictures amusingly grouped together, which the poor old folks, unable to read or too weak to do so, might turn over in the long days, during which they pass so many monotonous hours, and for which they will bless the clever busy fingers and kindly hearts, who in the midst of their own bright existence have remembered the poor and suffering.

Another mode of arranging pictures, which is a very good one for young children, is to paste them on a broad strip of holland, backed with coarse cloth, and bound with ribbon, which will roll up and tie with ribbon strings; it is strong, and not requiring to be turned over, cannot be torn, a great advantage for the tiny babies whose chubby fingers so eagerly and impatiently turn the leaves, eager to see "more."

Shawl or Wrap Case, for Travelling.

The case is of holland. It is bound all round with worsted braid. The border in embroidery may be in Andalusian wool or purse-silk. The roses and foliage

Fig. 114.

are cut out of cretonne, and fastened upon the holland with cording-stitch. The outlines of the pattern are in chain-stitch, or machine embroidery may be substituted. The straps are of holland, lined and embroidered with a simple design.

Pattern Embroidered on Leather,

FOR CIGAR-CASES, BOXES, PORTFOLIOS, ETC.

This pretty medallion design, when worked on leather, merino, or ribbed silk foundation, and with silk, curl cord, and gold, either in the same shade as the ground, or with the violet wreath in the centre, shaded after nature, makes an extremely tasteful finish for the inside of different small articles, such as mentioned, but when worked with a border and corners it can be used as an outer covering

Fig. 115.

for note-books, cigar-cases, etc., indeed, also as a centre for larger ones, such as glove-boxes, etc., etc.

Fan, with Net Embroidery.

The illustration shows an imitation lace intended to freshen up a much-used fan, when put over as a cover, or a plain silk one can be made more elegant by

Fig. 116.

applique lace flowers sewn on; the lace pattern can be worked without any great difficulty, and at small cost; round the outer edge of the fan is a pretty wreath of leaves and flowers. Flowers dispersed at short distances over the foundation can also be added if desired. When made on somewhat fine Brussels net, a paper foundation traced out with the pattern, is required; inside the outline parts the leaves of the sloping hole rows for the foundation are darned backwards and forwards with thread No. 300 taken double, and the flower parts worked in the round are to be filled up with chain-stitch; the outer sharp outlines, the veins and stalks, are made afterwards with fine glazed thread; in cutting away the net an edge of the same must be left, in order to be able to secure better the outer thread of the darned pattern. Very fine drilled silk for the leaves, and coarse, untwisted silk for the flowers, in place of the thread, give the effect of rich blond lace.

White Embroidered Tidy.

The charming little tidy shown in miniature in our illustration is exceedingly beautiful, as will be imagined from this sample.

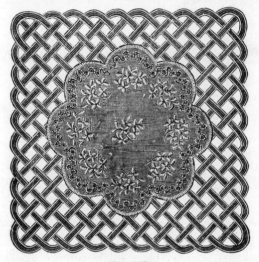

Fig. 117.

It is not made, as might be supposed, by applying a border of interlaced pieces around an embroidered centre, but by marking out an interlaced design, working the edges with buttonhole stitching, and cutting out the spaces between.

To do this, take a half yard of white linen or piqué, mark out a circular scalloped centre, with sprigs of leaves or sprays of small flowers in the centre of each scallop. These embroider in satin stitch, as also the border around the edge, buttonhole stitching the scallops. Then arrange the crossed-bar border as previously described. The tidy is extremely delicate, and when freshly laundried is peculiarly dainty and elegant looking

Corner of Design for Tidy, Etc.

Another exquisite piece of work of this kind is shown in the little corner-piece of Fig. 118, which is of tulle and fine Swiss muslin.

The design must be enlarged, of course, and consists of a foundation of the Swiss, upon which the lace is basted (on the parts required) in the centre and four corners. The design is then worked in chain stitching, and the Swiss cut away as usual from the lace, leaving the design upon the lace.

Fig. 118.

Such tidies are very much more artistic and refined in appearance than any woolen crocheted or Berlin work on canvas, as they may always be washed, and thus kept clean and fresh.

Fig. 119.   Fig. 120.

Borders for Square Tidies and Point for an Eight-Sided One.

Figs 119 and 120 show pretty borders for square tidies, and Fig. 121 a point for an eight-sided one. These are full-size, and will show the styles of work to the uninitiated. This work is extremely beautiful worked in colored silks or split zephyr.

Fig. 121.

Tidy of Serpentine Braid and Crochet Work.

Those of our readers who understand crocheting will at once see the method of applying the work in making the accompanying illustration (Fig. 122), which is one of the most beautiful tidies that can be made, and it will be found equally applicable for table-covers. The central square may be of different stitch entirely if desired; or a piece of embroidered Swiss or bobinet makes a lovely centre. We would also suggest the application of "tape-trimming," as it is called, made with fine linen tape as a substitute for the serpentine braid.

The border, which is clearly shown in the illustration, is put on around the centre, but will be better understood by examination than by any description we can offer. As these antimacassars are easily washed and ironed, they present many recommendations for ordinary use, and as may be imagined from the engraving (which is but a meagre representation of the model), is unusually beautiful in form and general appearance. A pretty change is made by lining the centre and catching the material around the inner edge of the border—the pink, blue or other bright color, surrounded by the white ornamented scallops, appearing exceedingly tasteful.

Fig. 122.—ANTIMACASSAR.

TABLE OF CONTENTS.

CHAPTER IV.—CANVAS WORK.

CHAPTER V.—BEAD WORK.

CHAPTER VI.—LACE WORK.

CHAPTER VII.—TATTING.

CHAPTER VIII.—KNITTING.

CHAPTER XVIII.—MISCELLANEOUS.